MW00639863

"*Superheroes Can't Save You* is creative, engaging, funny, and both biblically and historically accurate. Who could ask for more? Todd Miles takes familiar characters (especially for those of us who grew up on comics or watch movies) and skillfully uses them to help us better understand who Jesus is—and isn't. If we get it wrong about Jesus, in the end it won't matter much what else we get right. I'm happy to recommend this important and enjoyable book."

—**Randy Alcorn**, founder and director,
Eternal Perspective Ministries

"*Superheroes Can't Save You* is the most brilliantly creative Christology text I've ever read. By comparing each major Christological heresy to a familiar comic book superhero, and then contrasting them to the biblical Christ, Miles shows that each heresy presents a Jesus who is unable to do what the Bible claims Jesus did. As a result, the reader is given a lucid and memorable picture of the biblical Christ."

—**Bruce Ashford**, provost and dean of faculty,
Southeastern Baptist Theological Seminary

"In a world that is in desperate need for clarity on issues of faith, Dr. Todd Miles illuminates the truth about who Jesus is in a creative and compelling way. By combining his love for superheroes and his passion for the gospel of Christ, this book will engage a broad spectrum of readers as they journey through historic heresies that have plagued the church and are presented with the truth of who Jesus is. This is a fun read!"

—**Aaron Coe**, executive director, Passion Global Institute,
and assistant professor of world missions and intercultural
studies, Dallas Theological Seminary

"There are not many books that combine deep theology with insightful creativity, but *Superheroes Can't Save You* does, and does so brilliantly. In a world searching for something bigger and better with every movie ticket, Miles shows us how each superhero undersells what only the Son of God can truly provide. This is a book you will want to read for yourself, read with your kids, give to your youth minister, then to your pastor, and then to your friends. You will want to because it is a timely and accessible work and, more importantly, it offers us a Savior bigger and better than anything Marvel and DC has to offer—a Savior who can truly save us."

—**J. Ryan Lister**, associate professor of theology, Western Seminary, and director of doctrine and discipleship, Humble Beast

"*Superheroes Can't Save You* is a book that is culturally relevant, theologically astute, and capable of providing the reader with smiles as well as solid biblical knowledge. Youth and youth workers who disciple them will find this to be a very accessible book to promote the knowledge of our beautiful Savior."

—**Ron Marrs**, associate professor of youth and pastoral ministries, Western Seminary, and director, Portland Youth Workers Network

"I like superheroes. I love Jesus a lot more. It's not often that I'm able to bring the two together. In *Superheroes Can't Save You*, Todd Miles deploys some of the most iconic figures from the Marvel and DC universe to help us think rightly about the true story of history's greatest hero. This book teaches big truths in a fun way."

—**Russell Moore**, president, The Ethics and Religious Liberty Commission of the Southern Baptist Convention

"Who is Jesus? And who have people made Him out to be? In this engaging and insightful volume, Todd Miles clearly and faithfully unpacks the historic and biblical Christian understanding of Jesus, and compares it to familiar superheroes. Creative, fresh, and thoroughly biblical."
—**Christopher W. Morgan**, dean and professor of theology, School of Christian Ministries, California Baptist University

"Speaking both as a theology professor and a self–professed comic geek, I can't say enough good things about *Superheroes Can't Save You*. This is a brilliant example of contextual, pedagogical theology expressed in the vernacular of pop culture. Miles takes the content of historical theology that is so often prone to boring exposition and makes it accessible to students of all ages in an entertaining and engaging way. Highly recommended!"
—**Rhyne Putman**, associate professor of theology and culture, New Orleans Baptist Theological Seminary, and pastor of preaching and vision, First Baptist Church, Kenner, Louisiana

"It is rare to find someone who can take complex concepts and make them simple to comprehend. Yet it is here that Dr. Miles shines. One of the most central doctrines of Christianity is the nature of the second person of the Trinity, and this book makes it accessible to all. This book will also move your heart to love and worship Jesus Christ. As an added bonus, Dr. Miles' childhood stories and wry sense of humor will keep you captivated all the way through. The comic book metaphor is not just for kids—it's the key to understanding Christology for all ages and walks of life. I consider it a 'must read' and will highly recommend it to the women who attend our events."
—**Katherine Roberts**, co–founder and co–director, The Verity Fellowship

SUPERHEROES CAN'T SAVE YOU

SUPERHEROES CAN'T SAVE YOU

EPIC EXAMPLES OF HISTORIC HERESIES

TODD MILES

B&H
ACADEMIC

NASHVILLE, TENNESSEE

To Julius, Vicente, and Marcos
May you find in the Lord Jesus Christ, the one by whom,
through whom, and for whom you were made, the fulfillment
of all your deepest desires.
Colossians 1:15–20

CONTENTS

Acknowledgments   xiii
Introduction: As We Begin . . .   1

CHAPTER 1   9
Superman Can't Save You: The Dangers of Docetism
Jesus Was God in Disguise

CHAPTER 2   29
Batman Can't Save You: The Liability of Liberalism
Jesus Was Just a Remarkable Human

CHAPTER 3   53
Ant-Man Can't Save You: The Menace of Modalism
Jesus Was One of Three "Costumes" of the One God

CHAPTER 4   75
Thor Can't Save You: The Risks of Arianism
Jesus Was Created by God

CHAPTER 5   97
Green Lantern Can't Save You: The Agonies of
Adoptionism
Jesus Was a Good Man Adopted by God

CHAPTER 6   123
The Hulk Can't Save You: The Perils of Apollinarianism
  Jesus Had a Divine Mind in a Human Body

CHAPTER 7   151
Spider-Man Can't Save You: The Tyranny
  of Eutychianism
  Jesus Was Part Man and Part God

Last Words   177
Epilogue: Unfinished Business   183
Scripture Index   185
Subject Index   191

ACKNOWLEDGMENTS

This book was fun to write! I was able to combine my love for the Lord Jesus Christ with my childhood (and beyond) fascination with comic book superheroes.

The ideas and illustrations used throughout have been taught, tested, proven, modified, and often supplied by my students at Western Seminary over the past 14 years. I count it an undeserved privilege and immense joy to teach the glorious doctrine of the Lord Jesus Christ to current and future ministers of the gospel.

Dr. Gerry Breshears and Dr. Bruce Ware, my professors and mentors, have had more influence on my understanding of Jesus Christ than any other. How do you express gratitude for a gift like that? I believe that I first heard the Superman analogy from Gerry.

I had a great team of people, including my faculty colleagues, students, family, and friends, who voluntarily researched, read, and edited the chapters of this book. That team included Dr. Ryan Lister, Katie Roberts, Dr. Ron Marrs, Ethan Miles, Joshua Jen, Jerry Schoon, Levi Miles, Autumn Fabel, Tim Harmon, Drew Holmes, Ryan Dillon, Natalie Miles, Charlotte Roberts, and Grace Roberts.

I first taught this material at my home church, Hinson Baptist Church, to the Mariners Sunday school class. It was a ten-week series attended by teenagers through octogenarians, and their reaction made me think there just might be a book in this after all.

I also took the content for a test-drive at the East by Northeast youth retreat. I am thankful for the good feedback and enthusiastic response of Tyler Walsh and the youth groups of New Hope Community Church in Hermiston, Stanfield Baptist Church, Bethel Baptist Church in Milton-Freewater, First Baptist Church in La Grande, Prairie Baptist Church in Prairie City, Union Baptist Church in Union, and Faith Baptist Church of Harney County in Burns.

A special thank-you must be given to my friend and agent, David Sanford. His encouragement and legwork were crucial to the completion of this project.

I am grateful for my friends at B&H Academic, particularly Chris Thompson, Jim Baird, Audrey Greeson, Sarah Landers, and Jennifer Day for believing in this project enough to work with me and publish it.

My wife, Camille, is the glue that holds our crazy family together. She makes our home my favorite place on earth. Camille creates the space and opportunity for any worthwhile thing that I do; this book is no exception.

My older children played a unique role in this book. Not only did Ethan, Levi, and Natalie proofread the chapters; they also accompanied me in the "scholarly research" of attending superhero movies. Not every father has kids with whom he really likes to hang out (and who are willing to reciprocate in kind). The Lord has been exceedingly kind to me through them.

My youngest boys, Julius, Vicente, and Marcos, were also vital. All that time playing Batman and reading and watching the stories was not just fun; they were helping me write a book! It is with hope and love that I dedicate this book to them.

INTRODUCTION: AS WE BEGIN . . .

*G*rowing up, I had an absolute treasure trove of comic books, all collected during the '70s and early '80s. I was captivated by the world of the superhero and could not get enough. My parents gave me a modest allowance for the less-than-modest amount of work that I did around the house (usually mowing the lawn), and the money went almost entirely to my growing collection of comics. One of my favorite memories is walking to our local drugstore with a single dollar in my pocket. The possibilities, situated on the comic book rack, seemed endless. I could buy regular comics for a quarter apiece, or I could invest in a double volume, something like *Superman Family*, for 60 cents or so. No matter how long the choice took, it was certain that I would peruse through everything on the rack, reading most of them while I stood there, finally settling on just the right selection. Looking back, I am amazed that the drugstore owner was so patient. I was never reminded, "This is not a library!" I was never chastised for loitering. Perhaps because they knew that I would be buying something. It was inevitable. I had to make a purchase because that comic would be read and reread and reread.

My favorite superhero was the Flash. (I lived under the delusion that I was superfast, so I naturally gravitated toward that hero. I was disabused of that fantasy when I ran junior high track.) Following the exploits of the speedy Barry Allen opened the doors to more and more superheroes. Soon I was on my way to Smallville, Metropolis, and Gotham City, collecting a large number of *Superman* and *Batman* comics as well. Though partial to the DC world, I was no stranger to the Marvel universe. I had a good collection of *Spider-Man*, *Captain America*, and *Fantastic Four* comics. Some in my collection were first editions (*Superman Family* and *Man-Bat*, to name a couple).

Possessing these fantastic works of illustrated joy did not always work to my advantage. My collection was the envy of the neighborhood, and it was often a distraction. Friends would get lost at my house for hours, prompting their mothers to come and pull them out of the boxes of comics into which they had climbed. Whenever my cousins would come to town, I knew they would soon be found in my bedroom, poring through my treasure chests full of comic gold. Not realizing, and probably not caring, that they might be valuable someday, I read those comics to literal pieces. And when I went away to college, my mother threw them all away.

Every single one of them.[1]

But that is not the most important thing about me.

The most important thing about me is that I am a follower of Jesus. I first heard the gospel of Jesus Christ as a child, and I became a Christian at a young age, though I cannot tell you exactly when. I went to church every Sunday and lived a largely stagnate Christian life, staying out of trouble, but not really maturing much.

---

[1] She did the same thing with my baseball cards. You will be happy to know that my mother and I are doing fine. I did not know any better than she did that they could have become collector's items.

And then I went to college. Most people would not choose a secular school like Oregon State University to get serious with the Lord, but that is what I did, and in God's kindness, it was all part of his plan for me. I got involved with a campus ministry (the Navigators) that changed my heart and my life. Bible study was a joy, working with others for Christ's kingdom became my passion, and Jesus grew in magnitude in my understanding and life. I became convinced, and still am, that Jesus Christ is the most compelling, interesting, and remarkable person who ever lived. He is exactly who he claimed to be, precisely who the Bible teaches that he is—God in the flesh, the King of kings and Lord of lords. He owns me because he created me, died for me, bought me, and reigns over me. In every way possible, I owe him my life.

I went on to attend seminary and then later to teach at Western Seminary in Portland, Oregon. I love every minute of my job (except grading papers and attending faculty meetings). I get to work with and teach people committed to Christ and willing to serve him wherever he would have them go. It is fantastic.

And I still love comic books.

Superheroes are still a lot of fun, whether their stories are told in print, cartoons, television dramas, or movies. I have enjoyed almost all of them: the Avengers, Iron Man, Thor, Ant-Man, Superman, Batman, Spider-Man, Arrow, the Flash, Daredevil—television and movie content lately has been a comic lover's dream.

But I have not just been amused and entertained. I have also been paying attention and have realized that there is something in the world of superheroes that transcends mere escapism. The superheroes represent humankind's best efforts to create saviors, demigods made in our own image, beings who are able to rescue us from the horrors that accost us all as humans. The thing is, our best attempts to create such heroes fall desperately short of what we actually need. Superman, the greatest of the superheroes, is, well, super, and he is fantastically able to save imaginary people caught in the crosshairs of fictional crime. But even if he were real, he would not be able to save us from ourselves. He might be able to save individuals, but what of all humanity? Superman would not be able to rescue us from our greatest problems, and he certainly would not be able to deliver us from the wrath of God. He is not super enough, not human enough, not compassionate enough, and not divine in any way. He just does not measure up to the one who is more than enough of all those things, Jesus. Superman is no Jesus, and he never will be. The same is true of all the other comic book heroes. They just don't measure up.

Here is the thing: Jesus is the only one who can save us, but humans, darkened by sin and rebellion, don't like that fact. People know things are not quite right; in fact, they know things are nowhere close to right. We have all been there. We know, deep in our hearts, that we need someone to rescue us from the mess that we have made of our lives, our relationships, and the world around us. We know we need a Savior. But many people just don't want Jesus to be that Savior. Not the Jesus portrayed in the Bible. Not the actual living Jesus. The real Jesus asks too much, is too much, and says too much for their liking. So what are they to do?

Given that the list of potential saviors is pretty short, one solution throughout history has been to change and modify who Jesus is. Now, we can't actually affect the real, living Jesus by thinking wrongly about him. He is who he is, whether we like it or not. But we can deny things about Jesus—attributes, characteristics, abilities, and so on. I am sure you have seen this happen. People will often lie about themselves in their quest to be popular. Just a quick altering of facts to make themselves more likable. That is not a good route to go, but it is a road often traveled. It becomes a very dangerous road, the fast lane to certain destruction, when we do that to Jesus.

The bad ideas about Jesus throughout history, the subtle changing of who Jesus is here and there, all make Jesus less remarkable, less magnificent, and less of a Savior. In fact, it makes him no Savior at all. According to the logic and story of the Bible, *it takes everything that Jesus is and does to save us.* Any alteration of Jesus, no matter how small, turns him into someone who cannot rescue humanity, who cannot re-create the cosmos, and who cannot reign over it as the great sovereign King.

The bad ideas about Jesus, at least the popular bad ideas, don't turn him into an evil monster. No, they are just subtle changes or misunderstandings about the Lord that make him more comprehensible, more domesticated, less intrusive, and less demanding. But the Jesus created by these bad ideas cannot save.

And here is what I have discovered: *Every bad idea about Jesus can be illustrated by a superhero.* The most popular bad ideas about Jesus that have really challenged the church, that have caused Christian leaders to gather together in what we call "councils" to study and hammer out what the truth actually is, are all now embodied by one popular superhero or another. Every one of them. And that is a remarkable fact.

Here is why: it tells me that Jesus is better than anything that we could ever make up!

The superhero creators and writers did not and do not set out to create false saviors who will lead the world astray. They are writers of fiction whose goal is both to entertain and to teach by making up characters with incredible powers, who will fight for a fictional world that is supposed to mirror our own. The comic hero is meant to capture our imaginations. The writers' hope is that you will put yourself in the comic world and find in each of their heroes a champion that you wish actually existed in our own. Who hasn't read a comic and wished that Batman actually existed and watched over the streets, not of Gotham City, but of your hometown? Who hasn't daydreamed that Superman was actually patrolling the skies over your neighborhood, swooping in to fight injustice when it rears its ugly head?

And isn't it interesting that the best they can do is make up a character that looks suspiciously like a deficient view of Jesus?

We can't even make up anyone as wonderful as Jesus!

I have been teaching about Jesus for more than a decade now, and at times it has been difficult for my students to understand and remember the historical bad ideas about Jesus. It is worth studying them, because in looking at the faulty ideas of Jesus, the reality of Jesus becomes clearer. Students might not know or care about Docetism or Apollinarianism, but most people have heard of Superman and the Incredible Hulk. Illustrating these teachings with superheroes has made the topics more understandable and more fun. That is the primary reason why I have written this book: to help us understand and worship Jesus better.

WHY HERESY IS IMPORTANT

The theological term for "bad idea about Jesus" is *heresy*. Though some people think that anybody who disagrees with them about anything related to theology is a heretic, I think we should be more careful with the term. A bad idea or false teaching is a heresy if it undercuts the gospel. So for our purposes, if the bad idea about Jesus is such that the proposed Jesus could not do what the real Jesus actually did in order to save us, then that bad idea is a heresy. Every bad idea covered in this book undercuts the gospel. Thus, the proposed Jesus embodied in the superheroes cannot save anyone. Therefore, I have no problem referring to these bad ideas as "the Superman heresy" or "the Batman heresy."

As fun as the superhero illustrations might be, we are dealing with serious and deadly ideas. So another reason I am writing this book is to warn you. We will look back in time at the historical origin of each of the superhero heresies. I want you to know how you, if you are a Christian, can unwittingly fall into the Superman heresy or the Spider-Man heresy. There are people who have decided to believe in and worship someone closer to a fictional superhero than the actual Jesus Christ of the Bible and of history. And many of those people earnestly believe they are following the real Jesus! But they are not.

Finally, we will consider why any of this is important. These sections are crucial because if Jesus is to be able to do everything that the Bible says he does, then he has to be everything that the Bible says he is, without any alteration.

Each chapter takes on a different bad idea (or heresy) about Jesus, and each one of these heresies is embodied in a different superhero. I suppose you could look at it as a series of battles: Jesus versus Batman, or Jesus versus Ant-Man.[2] So the chapters will provide an explanation of each superhero; they will examine how each superhero represents a deficient view of Jesus; and they will demonstrate how Jesus is much better than the idea embodied in each superhero.

In all, I cover seven significant bad ideas about Jesus (and therefore seven different superheroes, if you are counting such things). The first two chapters establish the full humanity and full deity of Jesus Christ. The remaining chapters investigate how Jesus could be fully human and fully divine at the same time. I finish up with a final look at who Jesus actually is and how he could be everything that the Bible says he is.

---

[2] Remember, though: I like all of these comic superheroes!

I am certain that Jesus Christ is not only the most remarkable and important person ever, but he is the most remarkable and important person *for you*. The Bible makes the claim that "all things have been created through him and for him" (Col 1:16). That includes you and everybody you know, everybody who has ever and will ever exist. What this means is that every legitimate ultimate desire that you have can only be fulfilled in Jesus. Do you want significance? It can only be found in him. Do you want meaning? Follow Jesus—he will give it to you. Do you want life, true life, a life that is ultimately indestructible? It belongs to Jesus to give. Do you want a family? Jesus has made your adoption into the family of God possible. Do you want to be part of a team, a league? Jesus will give you a church. Do you want a purpose, a mission? Jesus promises to use you in his quest to save and re-create the world. Do you tire of trying to live up to what you think are God's impossible standards? Jesus offers to give you rest. Do you want to be forgiven—finally, once and for all? Forgiveness such as that can only be found in Jesus Christ. You were made to worship and serve him. Jesus is a good Shepherd and a great King, the greatest that could ever be. There is no one else.

My prayer is that as you read this, your understanding and appreciation of the gospel will grow and that you will marvel at the Lord Jesus Christ, fully human, fully divine, the King of kings and Lord of lords, our model for living, our Creator and Redeemer, our great High Priest, our help in temptation, and our wonderful Savior. To him be the glory forever and ever.

Now, let's get started.

1

SUPERMAN CAN'T SAVE YOU

| THE DANGERS OF DOCETISM | JESUS WAS GOD IN DISGUISE |

Your name is Kal-El. You are the only survivor of the planet Krypton. Even though you've been raised as a human, you are not one of them. You have great powers . . .

—Jor-El in the motion picture *Superman* (1978)

Now listen: You will conceive and give birth to a son, and you will name him Jesus. He will be great and will be called the Son of the Most High, and the Lord God will give him the throne of his father David. He will reign over the house of Jacob forever, and his kingdom will have no end.

—the angel Gabriel to Mary (Luke 1:31–33)

W hen I was young, I had a fascination with telephone booths,[1] largely because of the number of Superman

---

[1] For all you millennials out there who do not remember phone booths, they were three-by-three-by-eight-foot cubicles, each containing a phone, that

comics I had read. You remember Superman's MO. Whenever a crime was being committed in his vicinity, he would run to the nearest phone booth to shed his suit and tie, revealing his Superman cape and clothes underneath. He would then fly out to save the day. I remember peeking into such booths, hoping against hope that I would see a discarded suit and tie, proof positive of the existence of Superman. I often wondered how many suits Clark Kent went through, and what people thought when they came upon an abandoned but perfectly good suit of clothes in the phone booth. The homeless in Metropolis must have been well-dressed!

Let's pretend, for the sake of illustration, that you did find a suit and tie in a telephone booth, proving that the comic book world is real and that Superman does exist. Now, let me ask you a critical question: Was there a human being named Clark Kent?

The answer is . . . no. The human being named Clark Kent did not actually exist. Clark Kent is Superman's alter ego, but he is not a human being. Clark Kent is really just Superman in disguise. According to Superman lore, Superman was born Kal-El on the planet Krypton. His biological father, Jor-El, in an effort to save his son's life, jettisoned him from Krypton shortly before the planet exploded. The space vessel crash-landed on planet Earth near the small rural town of Smallville, Kansas, where the baby Kryptonian was found by Jonathan and Martha Kent. The Kents raised Kal-El as their own, giving the child the name Clark.

By all appearances, Clark seemed like any other human boy, but his adoptive parents knew better. They saw their child perform superhuman feats of strength on the family farm, away

---

used to be all over every city in the United States. If that does not help, picture this: a phone booth was the mechanism that Harry Potter used to get to the Ministry of Magic.

from the gaze of others. If the fact that the Kents had found Clark in a crash-landed rocket ship was not enough to tip them off, their young son hoisting tractors around the farmstead probably convinced them that Clark was no ordinary boy.

Jonathan Kent, Clark's adoptive father, looms large in the Superman narrative. He models and teaches the young Clark such virtues as charity, compassion, righteousness, and nobility. He teaches him about justice while pointing him toward his ultimate destiny, which was to use his superhuman powers for the common good. Mr. Kent also teaches the young Clark to blend in with others, to appear as normal as possible. For if Clark is to maximize his impact on the world, he must appear to be an ordinary human, no different from anybody else. Clark learns those lessons well and incorporates traits into his persona that are almost the opposite of who he truly is—acting the part of a clumsy, bookish young man. No one would ever suspect that Clark Kent is the future Man of Steel.

After graduating from Smallville High and having kept his true identity secret, Clark moved to Metropolis. The big city is the ideal place to fight crime as Superman, while still maintaining his seemingly human alter ego. Strategically taking a job as a reporter with a newspaper, the *Daily Planet*, Clark is ideally positioned to be quickly alerted of criminal activity. To all appearances, Clark is nothing more than a mild-mannered reporter. Certainly, at least initially, his coworkers, Lois Lane and Jimmy Olsen, do not suspect that the still clumsy and rather nerdy Clark Kent is actually Superman in disguise.

But that is exactly what Clark Kent is. Clark Kent is just a persona, a costume, a charade, that conceals the reality beneath the facade. Clark Kent trips and falls. He is not strong enough to do the simplest of acts. He gets tired and sick, often feigning exhaustion from overexertion. And when danger threatens, Clark Kent cowers and runs away (usually to the nearest phone

A lot of Christians view Jesus as Superman... WRONG.

booth to shed the suit and tie). But it is all an act. Superman is the most powerful being on the face of the earth. He is, as we well know, "faster than a speeding bullet! More powerful than a locomotive! Able to leap tall buildings in a single bound."[2] He is not weak. He is not clumsy. He is not foolish. And he is not afraid. Not one bit. He is, in every sense of the name, Superman!

Did you know that many in the church, both now and in the past, have the same idea about Jesus? Some read the Gospels in the Bible and dismiss all the talk of the humanity of Jesus, because Jesus was really "God in disguise." There was no human named Jesus, not really. That was just a persona, a costume, a charade, that concealed the reality beneath the disguise. Jesus just appeared to be human. He just *seemed* to be a man.

Is this your picture of Jesus?

Stronger than demons! Craftier than a Pharisee! Able to clear out temples with a single whip!

Look! Up on the mount. It's Moses! It's Elijah! It's Son of God-Man! Yes, it's Son of God-Man—strange visitor from up above, who came to Earth with powers and abilities far beyond those of mortal men. Jesus Christ—who can walk on water, multiply a few loaves and fishes into a meal for thousands, and who, disguised as Jesus of Nazareth, mild-mannered itinerant preacher from Galilee, fights a never-ending battle for truth, righteousness, and the kingdom of God!

I suspect that many Christians, even well-meaning ones, may have this exact notion of Jesus. But it's actually far from what the Bible reveals to us about Jesus. Now, many Christians are very good at arguing for (and rightly so) the deity of Jesus

[2] "Adventures of Superman (1952–1958) Quotes," IMDb, accessed June 22, 2017, http://www.imdb.com/title/tt0044231/quotes.

Christ. We believe that Jesus Christ was absolutely and fully God. Unfortunately, we are often so adamant about affirming the deity of Jesus that we ignore or even discount his humanity. I would go so far as to say that many Christians today do not know what to make of the humanity of Jesus. After all, how can humanity and deity coexist in one person anyway? We know that Jesus was the Son of God. Perhaps, like Superman, he just *seemed* to be human. Such thinking, though well-intentioned, is dead wrong. I call it the Superman heresy, but it has been around a long, long time.

THE HERESY

The early church was quick to recognize the deity of Jesus. But it was not long before the question arose, how can Jesus be both human and divine at the same time? Obviously, one very easy way to answer that is to deny that such a combination is even possible. Eliminate either the true humanity or true deity of Jesus and there is no more difficulty. And if you are committed to the deity of Christ, then you really only have one option: deny that Jesus was ever actually human. Oh, sure, Jesus might have *looked* like a human, but he wasn't really. Jesus only *seemed* to be human. Much like the way Clark Kent wore glasses, a suit, and a tie, his human disguise, so Jesus wore the first-century garb and disguise of humanity. The church eventually called this way of thinking *Docetism*, from the Greek word *dokein*, meaning "to seem."

Why would such an idea enter into the theology of the early church, and why would it gain any traction at all? The answer lies in understanding the world of the church in the first and second centuries. That world had been strongly influenced by Greco-Roman philosophy. A prominent teaching, based loosely on Platonic dualism, was the radical ethical and essential separation between the spiritual and the material. To the dualist, the material world was ignoble, shameful, and evil, while the spiritual world was noble, pure, and good. Not every Roman citizen of the first century shared this view, but enough did that such thinking quickly wormed its way into the young church. Dualism was such an issue that the apostle John had to go out of his way to affirm the humanity and physicality of Jesus to the early church:

> What was from the beginning, what we have heard, what we have seen with our eyes, what we have observed and touched with our hands, concerning the word of life—that life was revealed, and we have seen it and we testify and declare to you the eternal life that was with the Father and was revealed to us—what we have seen and heard we also declare to you . . . (1 John 1:1–3)

In this passage, John tells his Christian readers that he was an eyewitness to the incarnation of the Son of God. You can almost hear John saying, "Jesus really was human. He really walked the earth. I saw him. I touched him with my very own hands. It is this very human, very real Jesus that we preached to you." John was adamant: Jesus really did come in the flesh.[3]

Docetism later got a big boost from a false teaching that crept into the early church, called Gnosticism. (In fact, many believe that John's and even Paul's New Testament letters addressed early forms of Gnosticism.) Gnosticism was a syncretistic (or

---

[3] Church history tells us that John, in his later years at Ephesus, opposed a false teacher named Cerinthus, who was spreading the false doctrine of Docetism. There is a great story of John fleeing a Roman bathhouse when he spotted Cerinthus through the steam. John feared that God would destroy the bathhouse in righteous judgment upon the heretic Cerinthus, and he did not want to get hurt in the collateral damage. So I guess that Roman bathhouses are OK, as long as heretics are not sharing the space.

Mulligan stew-like) religion,[4] borrowing and combining ele-
ments of Greco-Roman philosophy and religion, Christianity,
and Judaism. Gnosticism's core tenet was that a secret knowledge (*Gnōsis*) was necessary for salvation, and that God, who
was good and spiritual, could have no direct interaction with
the material world. The goal of humanity was to escape the con-
fines of the material world, both now (through rigid asceticism)
and in the life to come. A full-blown Gnosticism did not arrive
on the scene until the second century, but Docetism, an essential
part of Gnosticism, had arrived in the church much earlier.

Now, this kind of dualism, the teaching that the material is
inherently evil and the spiritual is inherently good, is *completely
at odds* with biblical Christianity. The Bible teaches that God
created the world directly, speaking it into existence (Genesis
1). He created Adam and Eve in his image, *imago Dei*, and an
essential part of Adam and Eve was their bodies. This does not
mean that God has a body. Jesus was clear that God is Spirit
(non-corporeal); he has no body (John 4:24), but when God created man and woman in his image, he gave them bodies. I suspect this was to enable the first man and woman (and all others
after them) to image (or represent) God in this world the way
he wanted it done. Just as importantly, the Bible teaches that
an essential aspect of our salvation is the resurrection of our
bodies. The destiny of saved humanity is to dwell in the presence of God forever, and we will do so with real material bodies
(1 Cor 15:35–49). These will be new bodies, again designed, I
believe, to do those things that the Lord wants done in the new
heavens and new earth. But such biblical truths did not stop
the false teachers, and by the late first century, some churches

---

[4] Mulligan stew is a dish made from whatever ingredients are available. I
don't know who came up with the idea. I do know that it was served in elementary school cafeterias all through my childhood.

were infiltrated by those who claimed that the true Son of God could never have had an actual, physical body. Jesus could not have actually been human. He only seemed to be so. Just like Superman.

WHO COMMITS THE SUPERMAN HERESY TODAY?

Do we think of Jesus the same way? I suspect that there are not many card-carrying Docetists out there (if you meet any, please let me know). Very few people today would go so far as to deny that Jesus was really human. In our Western world, where naturalism holds sway at the philosophical and scientific levels,[5] you are more apt to find those who would deny that Jesus was supernatural and divine. But I am concerned that some Christians, without thinking, will lapse into the Superman heresy when they consider how Jesus did the things that the Bible tells us he did.

We can fall into the trap easily. It happens every time we assume that when Jesus was confronted with a difficult issue, be it temptation, sickness, demon possession, or the like, he overcame the obstacle by virtue of his deity. It is almost as if we think that when Jesus was tempted by Satan in the wilderness, he found the nearest telephone booth and pulled off his first-century Jewish robe, revealing the "Son of God-Man" insignia emblazoned on his chest. He then went off to do battle with Satan, laughing, "Who do you think you're kidding, deceiver? I am Son of God-Man! I cannot be tempted. Be gone!" and then,

---

[5] Naturalism is the worldview that teaches that the cosmos contains only matter, just atoms and molecules bouncing off other atoms and molecules. According to naturalism, there really are no spiritual or immaterial aspects to the cosmos.

using some sort of cool, divine superpowers, he vanquished Satan until the next episode. That is how all the *Superman* comics and television shows went. The seemingly feeble Clark Kent transforms into Superman and then easily defeats the bad guys. I wonder if some of us have the same idea of Jesus.

Of course, when we look in detail at the actual narrative of Jesus's temptations in a later chapter, we will find that Jesus did not do any of the things I just mentioned to stand against Satan. The means that Jesus used to battle the tempter were, well, quite ordinary. That is, they were common—the sort of tools that any human who loves the Lord could use.

A number of years ago, the "What Would Jesus Do?" (WWJD) movement was in full force. The idea behind it was that Christians (or anybody else, I suppose) who were faced with a difficult situation were to ask themselves, "What would Jesus do?" The question was supposed to bring clarity, insight, and guidance. For a while, you could not swing a tattered comic book without hitting someone wearing a WWJD bracelet, sporting a WWJD cap, eating from a WWJD lunchbox, doing schoolwork in a WWJD notebook—I could go on and on.

At any rate, Christians were supposed to stop in the moment of difficulty and ask, WWJD? I suppose there is some merit in asking the question. After all, the Bible teaches that Jesus left us "an example, that you should follow in his steps" (1 Pet 2:21).[6] But the entire WWJD enterprise was flawed from the beginning at various levels, and rather than being illuminated by the exercise, I often found it to be discouraging. Here is how it worked out with me.

[6] The WWJD movement is based on a book published in 1896 by Charles M. Sheldon, called *In His Steps: What Would Jesus Do?* The book took its title from Peter's words in 1 Pet 2:21.

Let's say I was in a sticky situation. Maybe I was battling a temptation and couldn't figure out how to beat it. Maybe I was trying to share the gospel with a friend and attempting to think up the right words to convince him of his need for Jesus. Or maybe I saw someone in desperate need, and I wanted to help that person. What to do? Ask, WWJD! But after pondering on what the risen and conquering Lord of the universe would do for a few moments, I usually came up with something like, "Jesus would laugh at Satan and say no to the temptation because he was the Son of God." Or, "Jesus would know the exact thing to say that would confound even the smartest Pharisee, because he was the Son of God." Or, "Jesus would multiply loaves and fishes into a feast. And he could do that because he was the Son of God." And then, growing discouraged, I would think to myself, *I can't do any of those things, because I am not the Son of God*. The question was absolutely no help. In fact, it actually made things worse.

And here's the thing: I was lapsing into the Superman heresy and I didn't even realize it. Jesus can be a help in temptation. He can guide us, teach us, and empower us, and we will discover why as the book proceeds. But the reason is not that Jesus is "Son of God-Man."

WHAT THE BIBLE SAYS

The Bible could not be clearer that Jesus was fully human. His humanity was prophesied long before his birth in Bethlehem. He was born like any other human (really!). He lived, grew, and did all the things that humans do.

Jesus Was Predicted by the Prophets. The prophets anticipated long before Jesus was born that God would work his salvific plans through a man who was to come.

Approximately 1,000 years before Jesus was born, David, the second king of Israel, had it in his mind to build a really nice temple for the Lord. David recognized that the Lord had blessed him in myriad ways, not the least of which was a fantastic palace that made the simple tent that housed the ark of the covenant of God look like, well, a simple tent (2 Sam 7:1–2). The Lord responded to David's offer by sending the prophet Nathan to tell him that rather than David building a house for him, the Lord would build a house for David. The Lord went on to say, "When your time comes and you rest with your fathers, I will raise up after you your descendant, who will come from your body, and I will establish his kingdom. He is the one who will build a house for my name, and I will establish the throne of his kingdom forever" (2 Sam 7:12–13). Theologians call this the Davidic covenant, and it is one of the most important events recorded in the Bible, because in the covenant God committed to work his plan of redemption in and through the house of David. The substance of the promise is that David would have a son who would eventually assume the throne and reign forever. That son would also build a temple for the Lord. Questions arise immediately: How can a son of David reign forever? What about David's son Solomon? Isn't he the fulfillment? Didn't he build the temple? Solomon did reign over a more prosperous kingdom than his father, and he did build a temple. But his reign did not last forever (he died), and the temple he built was destroyed (by the Babylonians in the 500s BC). The fulfillment awaited someone else, from the line of David, a future son. And that is what we need to emphasize: God's promise would be fulfilled by a boy being born, from the family of David. A human boy.

More than 700 years before Jesus was born, the prophet Isaiah predicted, "Therefore the Lord himself will give you a sign: See, the virgin will conceive, have a son, and name him Immanuel" (Isa 7:14). I grant you that this was going to be no ordinary baby. Clearly the conception of Jesus was absolutely remarkable, a one-of-a-kind sort of affair, but that does not mean that the virgin's baby would be anything less than human. The child would be called "Immanuel," meaning "God with us" (Matt 1:23), indicating that there was going to be something divine about the child as well. We will discuss the implications of the divinity of Jesus in the next chapter, and really for the rest of the book. But for now, recognize that it was predicted that a woman was going to give birth to a son. A boy. A human boy. Nothing in the prophecy suggests that he would be anything less than human. There is plenty to suggest that he would be more than your typical human, but he would not be less.

At about the same time that Isaiah was alive, the prophet Micah predicted that a great ruler would be born in Bethlehem (Mic 5:2–3). That ruler would "stand and shepherd them in the strength of the LORD, in the majestic name of the LORD his God" (v. 4). The baby born in Bethlehem would be great, but a great *human*.

There are other passages that could be considered (e.g., Isa 9:6; Dan 7:13), but they make the same point. The Lord had a plan to redeem his people. He announced it through his prophets centuries in advance. And that plan focused on a man. This prophetic anticipation is important because it demonstrates that Jesus's humanity was not an afterthought, an accident, or an ad hoc addition to God's master plan. As we will see, the humanity of Jesus is essential to God's saving purposes. To be sure, Jesus is a remarkable man. But he is truly a man.

Jesus Was Born and Grew Up Like a Normal Human. Luke recorded the birth of Christ in the second chapter of his Gospel. Anyone who has ever watched the *Peanuts* Christmas special

(*A Charlie Brown Christmas*) is well acquainted with Linus's famous reading of the passage. Because of a census decreed by Caesar Augustus, all people in the Roman Empire were to travel to their ancestral homes and register. Luke wrote:

> Joseph also went up from the town of Nazareth in Galilee, to Judea, to the city of David, which is called Bethlehem, because he was of the house and family line of David, to be registered along with Mary, who was engaged to him and was pregnant. While they were there, the time came for her to give birth. Then she gave birth to her firstborn Son, and she wrapped him tightly in cloth and laid him in a manger, because there was no guest room available for them. (Luke 2:4–7)

I want to point out that despite all the events that transpired before and after the birth (angel announcements, a virgin conception, traveling to register, giving birth in a stable, a multitude of angels singing, Magi visiting and worshiping, Mary and Joseph fleeing for their lives, the slaughter of infants—that is quite a list!), look at how simple Luke's account of the birth is. When it came time for Mary to deliver her baby, she gave birth just as every woman did at the time. There is nothing remarkable about the actual labor or delivery. It was a normal human birth, complete with blood, pain, tears, and joy in the end. Forget what we sing at Christmas in "Away in a Manger" about how "the little Lord Jesus, no crying he makes." I am sure that when the cattle woke up Jesus (or when he got hungry), he cried. Why? Because Jesus was a human baby, and human babies cry. If they don't, there is something wrong. Jesus's conception was remarkable and miraculous; the angelic activity was extraordinary; emissaries showing up from distant lands and shepherds arriving from nearby to worship must have been jaw-dropping (see Luke 2:8–19). But none of those things change the facts of Jesus's birth. It was the normal birth of a baby boy.

After that, Jesus grew up like a normal boy. In fact, his upbringing, save a flight to Egypt and later getting lost in Jerusalem, was so unremarkable that none of the Gospel writers have much to say about it. Luke summarized his boyhood this way: "And Jesus increased in wisdom and stature, and in favor with God and with people" (Luke 2:52). It is significant that Jesus grew in these ways. We see growth in godliness and early signs that Jesus was respected by people. But Jesus is portrayed by the Gospel writer as a godly human boy. People have not always been satisfied with such mundane reports about Jesus's early life. There has long been a hunger for extraordinary tales that prove Jesus was beyond human. About 100 years after the Gospels of Matthew, Mark, and Luke were written, the *Infancy Gospel of Thomas* was written. It contains all sorts of wild stories of the boy Jesus breathing life into clay birds, cursing troublesome neighbors with blindness, and even putting a bully to death (the bird story even made it into the Muslim Qur'an[7]). The stories are the stuff of fantasy and lack credential and the ring of truth. The church has never accepted them as authentic or truthful. But they do demonstrate how dissatisfied people are with an ordinary human boyhood for Jesus. When we are not thinking rightly, we want Jesus to tip his divine hand and do some magical act, like the young Clark Kent, as he hoisted tractors all over the Kent family farm. But we dare not fall prey to the Superman heresy. The Gospel writers present a very human Jesus to us, because he was just that, very human.

Jesus Demonstrated Normal Human Limitations. Part of the human experience is needing nourishment and rest, and Jesus was no exception. It might not seem remarkable to note,

---

[7] See Surah 5.110 if you want to check it for yourself.

but it is important: Jesus got hungry and thirsty, and he needed sleep. In Matthew 4, Jesus spent a remarkable amount of time praying and fasting. The result: he was hungry (v. 2). If we see Jesus as being fully human, we would expect that to be the case. But if Jesus is God-in-disguise, then there is no reason to think that he would get hungry. Why would he?

On another occasion, after a long day of preaching and healing, Jesus was so tired that he fell fast asleep on a boat that was taking him to his next destination (Matt 8:21–27). A storm arose on the Sea of Galilee that threatened to swamp the boat. The storm was so fierce that his disciples, many of whom were seasoned fishermen, feared for their lives. But Jesus was so exhausted that he slept through wind, waves, and water crashing over the sides of the boat. Now, I suppose this might have been an act. Perhaps if Jesus were God-in-disguise, it might be a trick to get the disciples to come to him for help. But the problem with this is that Matthew never said this. He simply relayed what happened—there was a crazy storm, and Jesus had to be awakened from a deep sleep. We can only conclude that the reason Jesus was asleep is that he was tired—just as any human would be after a hard day's work.

John's Gospel tells the story of Jesus and his disciples traveling through Samaria (4:1–44), where Jesus reached out to a Samaritan woman at a well. This passage is best known for Jesus's statement that God is seeking people who will worship him in Spirit and in truth (vv. 23–24). But don't miss the reason that Jesus initially spoke to the Samaritan woman. He stayed behind while the disciples went to get food because he was "worn out from his journey" (v. 6). He asked the Samaritan woman for something to drink because he was thirsty (v. 7). I suppose that Jesus could have pretended to be hot and thirsty, hoping to create an opportunity to speak to the woman. But that is not how John told his story. We would only think that if we had some precommitment to Jesus not really being human, a stubborn refusal to give up the Superman heresy.

Jesus Died. All four Gospels are adamant about this event in Jesus's life. When he was tacked to a Roman cross, he died. Jesus did not fake his death. He did not swoon. He was not even mostly dead. He was completely, 100 percent dead. The Roman soldiers, masters at administering death, oversaw the entire affair. The normal Roman crucifixion practice to hasten death was to break the legs of the victim, making it impossible for him to raise himself up on the cross to breathe. But Jesus, due to the beating and trauma he had endured leading up to the cross, was already spent. He died before the leg-breaking became necessary. Suspecting that Jesus was already dead, the Romans drove a spear into his side to confirm the fact. Sure enough—Jesus was dead. Here is the rub. God cannot die. But humans can and do. Jesus's death demonstrates that he was absolutely human.

WHY IS THIS IMPORTANT?

OK, so Jesus was human. So what? What is the harm in pretending that Jesus was actually God in disguise? Would it really impact anything? Yes. The stakes are incredibly high. The biblical story depends on the humanity of Jesus. He didn't just happen to be human. Jesus had to be human. If he wasn't human, then we lose nothing less than the gospel. And you and I, in turn, lose any hope of being saved. Here is how the gospel works only if Jesus is human.

In the beginning, God created the heavens and the earth (Gen 1:1). He also created everything in it, including the first humans. Those two, Adam and Eve, were the high point of creation, for they alone were created in the image of God. These image bearers were created to rule in God's place, exercising dominion over all that God had just made. Of course, it is a delegated authority. But God, as the Creator of everything, has creator's rights over everything that he has made. He, and he alone, has the right to delegate such authority, and he granted it to the first human pair, effectively saying, "Take care of my stuff." Such a responsibility is beyond generous, yet it is graciously granted.

You know what happened next. The joy of Genesis 1 and 2 was ripped apart by the rebellion of Genesis 3. God had granted to the first humans all that he had made, holding only one thing back for their own good. God told them that they could eat from any tree in the garden—they were all at Adam and Eve's disposal, save one—the tree of the knowledge of good and evil. This was no stingy God, selfishly and arbitrarily holding the best back. Adam and Eve could have all they wanted, except one thing. And that one thing came with a warning: Eating from that tree would bring death.

The punishment seems harsh until we consider the actual crime. Adam and Eve were God's vice-regents, the ones who ruled in his stead over all that God had made. The Lord had granted to Adam and Eve dominion over *everything* he had made. This human pair was God's crowning achievement. They represented God's rule on earth. Thus, their sin was not merely the picking of some forbidden fruit. It was rebellion, treachery, and betrayal. God's ambassadors had rebelled against him and brought upon themselves death, and upon the creation they had so mismanaged, a curse.

Human sin had brought this calamity, and human death, the penalty, was right at the center of it. Sin is a human problem. And a human problem requires a human solution. In fact, the Lord said that the offspring of the woman, a baby to be born—a human baby—would grow to crush the head of the serpent (Gen 3:15). In the midst of the cursing, the Lord articulated that humanity's only hope would be a human. But we find that humans were not able to take care of the problem. From Genesis 4 to the end of the Old Testament, we find failure after failure after failure on the part of humans to make things right, to reconcile themselves to God. Meanwhile, death, the just penalty of human sin, continued to reign. Look at Genesis 5 for proof. Those early humans lived a long time, but their end is the same—"then he died . . . then he died . . . then he died" (vv. 5, 8, and 11, among others). The drumbeat of death is relentless and terrifying, just like the drums of Moria beating out *doom, doom, doom* for the fellowship in *The Lord of the Rings*. There is no escape. Humans, the ones who got us into this mess and the ones rightfully tasked with getting us out, are singularly incapable of doing so.

In the midst of that Old Testament record of failure and death, we are introduced to a biblical paradigm that brings hope: "Salvation belongs to the LORD" (Jonah 2:9; Ps 3:8). This was not just an arbitrary statement, the description of the best man for the job. It was a prescription for how things must be— the prayer of a desperate humanity in a hopeless situation. If humanity was to be saved, God must step in. But how?

God initiated a plan first through a man (Abraham), and then through his extended family. He rescued that family from slavery in Egypt and made them into a nation (Israel), his treasured possession, a kingdom of priests who were to display the Lord's justice and mercy to the nations. Of course, the sin problem persisted, even for the Lord's people. So God introduced a sacrificial system. An animal could substitute for the people, a life for a life. Year after year sacrifices were offered, an endless progression. Although the Lord prescribed them, their continued use pointed to their lack of efficacy.

Imagine a Jewish family dutifully making their annual pilgrimage to Jerusalem for the Day of Atonement. In tow is a sheep or goat from the herd. I suspect there were many opportunities to talk on the road, and I bet that often the subject matter between father and children turned to why the family lamb had to be slaughtered. The answer was, "The lamb is being offered as a substitute for us, its life for ours." The obvious question that had to be asked was, "How can a sheep or goat take the place of a human?" and further, "How can the death of a sheep or goat atone for human sin?" And the answer, of course, is that it can't. Not only is a lamb not a human, but it is completely inferior to a human. It was a human, an image bearer, who had rebelled and incurred the penalty of death, and it would have to be an image bearer who would pay that price.

So, if sin is a human problem that requires a human solution and salvation belongs to the Lord, how can anybody be saved? The answer lies in the incarnation of the Son of God. Jesus is Immanuel, God *with* us. But Jesus is the son of David, a human *like* us. He could offer himself as a substitute for human sin because he is one of us. If Jesus was not truly and fully human, unlike Clark Kent, then he could not die for our sin. If he only seemed to be human, then there is no gospel, no good news. If Jesus is just "God in disguise," like Superman, we all stand hopelessly condemned.

Superman cannot save you. But Jesus can. Jesus can redeem us because he took on our flesh, our nature—he is one of us. But he is not merely one of us. He is God in the flesh. And that is equally important, as we will find out next.

Discussion Questions

Questions for Personal Reflection

- What are the personal benefits of the humanity of Christ?
- What goes through your mind when you read of Jesus getting hungry and tired?
- Do you see Jesus as "like you"? If not, why not?
- How has the humanity of Jesus inspired your love and devotion to Jesus?

Questions for Group Discussion

- Why will the gospel not work if Jesus is not fully human?
- Reread 1 John 1:1–3. Why was it so important to John that he had actually seen and touched Jesus?
- Describe a situation where someone talked of Jesus as though he were not really human.
- Have you ever thought that asking "What Would Jesus Do?" is silly because, after all, Jesus is God? If so, how might believing that Jesus is fully human change the way you approach temptation?
- What gets in the way of seeing Jesus as your legitimate and true example?

For Further Study

Read John 4:6–7 (from the story of Jesus's encounter with the woman at the well). Consider the implications of the fact that Jesus was actually hot, tired, and thirsty. How did such things help him in his interaction with the Samaritan woman?

2

BATMAN CAN'T SAVE YOU

THE LIABILITY OF LIBERALISM

JESUS WAS JUST A REMARKABLE HUMAN

I'm Batman!

> —*Batman* (1989)

I am the way, the truth, and the life.

> —Jesus (John 14:6)

*B*atman has always been a favorite of mine. I bought the comics, watched the cartoons, and went to the movies. From Michael Keaton to Ben Affleck, I have enjoyed them all (some more than others). I even appreciate the campy 1960s TV series starring the late Adam West (*BAM! KAPOW!*). To this day, a rainy Saturday afternoon seems to be a great time to sit with my twelve-, ten-, and nine-year-old sons and watch Batman duking it out with Cesar Romero's Joker.

I really like Batman. And I am not sure why.

Let's face it: When it comes to superhero credentials, Batman does not bring much to the table. He has no superpowers. He does not have the speed of the Flash. He cannot

breathe underwater, like Aquaman. He cannot turn into anything or anybody. He is not from another planet. If you add
Batman's strength to Superman's strength, you pretty much
end up with Superman's super-strength. It is almost comical
in comparison. Superman can fly faster than a speeding bullet. Batman has to run to his car (and always takes the time to
fasten the seat belt). Superman has X-ray vision. Batman has a
belt and bat-rope. (Holy unfair fights, Batman!) The attributes
of Superman are lauded in his theme song, while the best that
can be sung of Batman is "Nuh-nuh-nuh-nuh-nuh-nuh-nuh-
nuh, Batman!"

And yet still, who doesn't like Batman? Maybe it is because
Batman's character is developed better than that of any other
comic book hero. Batman is so human we can actually relate
to his dark and tortured world. Maybe it is the colorful cast
of villains that he fights—the Joker, the Riddler, the Penguin,
Catwoman. Those are some fun and interesting bad guys. But
enemies are not able to carry a superhero's popularity for long,
no matter how intriguing they might be.

Batman is cool; there is no doubt about that. The man in
the dark suit, cape, and cowl is the secret identity of Gotham
City businessman, philanthropist, and jet-setter Bruce Wayne.
The comics and latest movies are dark, reflecting the mood of
Gotham City and the difficult origin of Batman himself. Bruce
was the son of the physician and businessman Thomas Wayne
and his wife, Martha. As a child, Bruce witnessed his parents'
murder at the hands of a mugger and vowed to avenge them.
Now an adult and aided by Alfred, the faithful butler who
raised him, Bruce has dedicated himself to fighting crime and
cleaning up Gotham City.

Bruce Wayne certainly has resources—more than anybody
else imaginable. He is a billionaire with all the newest science

and technology advances at his disposal. Blessed with ninja fighting skills and able to marshal intimidation and fear against most of the criminals he fights, it is not as if Batman has nothing going for him. He even has a nifty utility belt loaded with all sorts of handy bat-gadgets.[1] Not quite the same as X-ray vision, but it will certainly do in a pinch.

But none of those things are superpowers. None are alien. None are supernatural. There is no hint that Batman is anything other than an incredible human being (with seemingly unlimited amounts of cash). Though such qualities and skills are never found in any one real human being (that is what makes him Batman, after all), they are just human qualities and skills. He may be the most remarkable human being in comic lore, but in the final analysis he is just a human being.

And some people feel the same about Jesus.

To these folk, Jesus is a remarkable human being, possessed of enormous charisma, wisdom, compassion, leadership qualities, and teaching ability. Jesus may be, and probably is, the most incredible human being who ever lived. It is entirely likely that there has never been, nor will there ever be, another man like Jesus. But in the final analysis, he was just a man. He is worthy of respect, but not reverence; admiration, but not adoration; emulation, but not exaltation. He is not divine in any unique way. He is a human being, and that is all.

I call the belief that Jesus Christ was just a human being and nothing more, the "Batman heresy." It has been around for a long time. As we will see, a merely human Jesus might seem cool and inspirational, but he cannot save you.

---

[1] Remember the Joker's memorable line in *Batman* (1989): "Where does he get those wonderful toys?"

THE HERESY

About 200 years ago, a German pastor and professor named Friedrich Schleiermacher (1768–1834) grew concerned that the church was losing numbers due to its antiquated beliefs. Thinking people, in his estimation, were no longer interested in Christianity because the claims of the Bible could not stand up to the tests of reason. Sophisticated people no longer believed in virgins giving birth, food being multiplied, resurrections, or any miracle for that matter. They certainly did not believe in something as outlandish as the incarnation, that God was born as a human in a Bethlehem stable. Perhaps in the superstitious past, uneducated people might have believed such nonsense, but not anymore. Not with the scientific revolution of the sixteenth through eighteenth centuries leading the way. Schleiermacher saw his educated friends leaving the church and making a mess of their lives. To his credit, he cared about his friends, but his advice was horrific.

In a book titled *On Religion: Speeches to Its Cultured Despisers*, Schleiermacher pleaded with his friends not to give up on Christianity. Sure, he argued, there might be some things that are impossible for "modern" people to believe, but don't throw the baby out with the bathwater. The miracles recorded in the Bible are not essential to Christianity. Religion, and the Christian faith in particular, is a feeling. He invited his friends to search their hearts, to inquire deep within their souls, and look for that inescapable feeling that there is something more out there, that humans are not self-sufficient, that we are ultimately dependent on something greater than ourselves for the many aspects of our existence. That feeling of ultimate dependence that everybody possesses to some degree is evidence that God exists. Embracing that feeling of ultimate dependence is to live in relationship with God.

The Christian Scriptures, according to Schleiermacher, were written by men who were deeply in touch with their sense of absolute dependence. The Bible, therefore, is an imperfect record of those who had experienced this God-consciousness. In other words, it was a record, in different literary genres (poetry, narrative, law, etc.) of their religious experiences. Those writers were products of their ancient times. They might very well have believed what they wrote, that food could be multiplied to feed thousands, that lame men could be made to walk, or that the dead could be raised. But they also might not have believed it. People in the modern era, who know better, are certainly not required to believe such things. That being the case, the Bible may be helpful, but it is not necessary. A person's faith and experience do not hinge on believing or even reading the Bible.

Schleiermacher is now known as the father of Christian Liberalism and, when it comes down to it, he was really the creator of a Batman-like Jesus. Schleiermacher believed that Jesus was a remarkable man. In fact, he was the most remarkable of men. He was one in whom human nature (particularly the spiritual and moral side) reached something close to perfection. There has never been a person so in touch with his God-consciousness. He was absolutely dominated by his sense of total dependence upon God. Therefore, he is worth listening to. His example is worth following. So radical was Jesus's example that the people of his day, particularly the religious establishment, could not understand or even tolerate him. They lashed out in violence and had him put to death on a Roman cross. His death is an example. But it was not substitutionary; that is, Jesus did not die in your place, taking a punishment that you deserved in order to reconcile you to God. And Jesus certainly was not God incarnate. That would be silly. Thinking people do not believe silly things. But according to Schleiermacher, the essence of Christianity, minus the supernatural and miraculous, minus the incarnation and substitutionary death of Jesus on a cross, is still the best thing going. Jesus was remarkable. He is worth emulating. But he was just a man. Much like Batman.

The Batman heresy was not limited to the 1800s. It is alive and well in our time. The most recent highly publicized instance of this was the so-called Jesus Seminar, which began in the late twentieth century.[2] Just like Schleiermacher, the Jesus Seminar has invented a Batman-like Jesus who is just a remarkable human, but nothing more.

The Jesus Seminar was composed of a group of liberal religious scholars active during the 1980s and 1990s.[3] Its purpose was to study the historical Jesus, rescuing him from the dogma of the church and the often misleading data of the New Testament. Perhaps the Jesus Seminar's most infamous "contribution" to the study of Jesus was their historical "assessment" of the historicity of the words of Jesus in the Bible. Each scholar used different colored marbles to communicate his confidence that the words of Jesus written in the New Testament were actually uttered by Jesus (red, pink, grey, and black for differing degrees of confidence that the saying or event described actually happened—I am not making this up). In the end, the Jesus Seminar concluded that less than 20 percent of the sayings attributed to Jesus in the four Gospels were something that Jesus *actually* said or even something *like* Jesus said.

---

[2] The actual impact of the Jesus Seminar is difficult to discern. In my opinion, its ability to promote and use the press far exceeded its actual contributions to the area of Jesus studies. The Jesus Seminar was the darling of the media, but rarely did the numbers or contributions warrant the attention they received.

[3] An example of the scholars involved in the Jesus Seminar were Robert Funk, founder of the Westar Institute; the Roman Catholic John Dominic Crossan of DePaul University; and Marcus Borg, professor of religious studies at Oregon State University.

With such low confidence in the historicity of the Gospels, it is not surprising that the Jesus Seminar concluded that Jesus was not divine, not born of a virgin, and did not possess supernatural powers. Rather, Jesus was an itinerant preacher and sage (many members of the Jesus Seminar have slightly different opinions) who was crucified by the Romans for political reasons (he was a disturber of the peace), and stayed dead once he was taken off the cross. He certainly did not get up from the dead. You might wonder what data the Jesus Seminar used to arrive at such conclusions. When the Bible is rejected as an accurate historical source and church documents are rejected for being too biased, the available information from other sources is a bit thin. In my opinion, their so-called quest for the historical Jesus was a giant exercise in question begging. When you deny the supernatural for philosophical and ideological reasons, and then reject any reference to the supernatural in the Bible on the basis that it "just can't be correct," it should not be surprising that all you are left with in the end is the kind of Jesus that the Jesus Seminar wanted to find in the first place. They might call it scholarship, but most people would call it "cooking the books."

This is not to say that the Jesus Seminar had no respect for the figure they created. In their estimation, their Jesus was a remarkable spiritual man who was wiser, more compassionate, and more discerning than perhaps any man who had ever lived. But in the end, he was just a remarkable man. In fact, the Jesus that the Jesus Seminar created is closer to Batman than to the Jesus revealed in the Bible. If I had to choose, I much prefer Batman to the Jesus concocted by the Jesus Seminar. But for my money, the real Jesus, the Jesus Christ who walked the earth and who is written about by those who gave eyewitness accounts of his words and deeds, is vastly superior to anything that anybody could possibly make up.

WHO COMMITS THE BATMAN HERESY TODAY?

Now, most of us have not spent a lot of time studying the works of Friedrich Schleiermacher. And though the Jesus Seminar has given a little academic muscle to some, their works are (thankfully) not widely read by those in or outside the church. But that does not mean that the Batman heresy is limited to a few in the academy and those who read dead nineteenth-century German theologians. On the contrary, believing that Jesus was just a man is probably the first and easiest heresy to fall into. Believing that the carpenter's son from Nazareth who preached to many and died on a Roman cross is easy. It takes no commitment and no faith. Believing that Jesus is merely human will cost you nothing. In fact, the merely-human Jesus is quite popular in our Western culture, and speaking poorly of Jesus is largely frowned upon. Insulting Jesus is received much as insulting Gandhi or Mother Teresa would be. Instead, "Jesus is my homeboy" T-shirts are popular. After all, the attributes of the human Jesus are the best of what we aspire to be—compassionate, merciful, kind, resolute, wise. We could go on and on. It is when people start talking about the deity of Jesus that things get sticky.

I mentioned earlier, when I described Schleiermacher's motivation, that he wanted his cultured friends to embrace Christianity, or at least his watered-down version of it. And for them to do so, the deity of Jesus (not to mention anything supernatural) had to go. It was an obstacle to their coming to Christ. After all, a historical figure who was remarkable but died and no longer lives poses no threat to the way anyone behaves or relates to God. Jesus might have said a few things that come in handy. He might be a decent role model to follow occasionally. He might even inspire some to live differently (as long as the cost is not too high). But the significance of a merely human Jesus ends once his memory escapes our minds.

For Christians who tire of being the object of ridicule, who are frustrated that they are not taken seriously in the marketplace of ideas, or who just want to avoid the eye rolls of those who think differently, it can be very tempting to find the common ground of Jesus as the great human teacher and leave it at that. No one will argue with you if all you say about Jesus matches the merely human Jesus of unbelievers' imaginations. A Batman-like Jesus will not offend anybody. Maybe you have friends whom you genuinely care for, but they just can't come to grips with a Jesus who is both human and divine. The desire to downplay Christ's deity can be huge, but don't go there. Beware the temptation to change the reality of who Jesus actually is to make him palatable for our "cultured" friends (or uncultured friends, for that matter). There are a few words that apply to those who change Jesus to make him more attractive to others—dishonest, idolatrous, and blasphemous. Remember that Jesus never did the "bait-and-switch" thing in calling people to him. Neither should we. He wanted people to count the cost, to go in with their eyes open (see Luke 9:23). He never once promised that following him would be easy. Fight the temptation to believe in and present a merely human Jesus. Failing to do so is dishonest and ultimately helps no one, least of all the people for whom you are trying to make Jesus appealing. A Batman-like Jesus cannot save you or anyone else. As we will see, the Jesus presented in the Bible is far from merely human, and his deity is absolutely essential if he is to be the Savior we need.

WHAT THE BIBLE SAYS

The Scriptures present a Jesus who is far from merely human, and they do so consistently throughout the Old Testament prophecies, through the chronicling of Jesus's life in the Gospels, and the New Testament letters that describe Jesus's life. The Bible

believer is left with no option but to affirm the deity of Jesus
Christ.

Old Testament Prophecies Spoke of Him. The prophet
Isaiah spoke of one who was to come who would be born, but
he would take the name "Immanuel," literally, "God with us"
(Isa 7:14). Just two chapters later, Isaiah gave us the majestic
prophecy that Handel put to music in his oratorio, *Messiah*:

> For a child will be born for us,
> a son will be given to us,
> and the government will be on his shoulders.
> He will be named
> Wonderful Counselor, Mighty God,
> Eternal Father, Prince of Peace.
> The dominion will be vast,
> and its prosperity will never end.
> He will reign on the throne of David
> and over his kingdom,
> to establish and sustain it
> with justice and righteousness from now on and forever.
> The zeal of the LORD of Armies will accomplish this.
>   (Isa 9:6–7)

Meditate on Isaiah's words. The prophet looked forward to a
baby being born who would be King over Israel. As we saw
in the previous chapter, he would be a son of David, a human,
and his reign would be remarkable, characterized at last by justice and righteousness. In fact, it is a reign that will never end.
Immortality is ascribed to this future King. And the reason is
clear. Somehow that baby to be born would be "Mighty God"
himself and is named as such. No wonder the reign of the great
King would be eternal.

Jesus and Others Claimed He Is Divine. The Gospels affirm
the Old Testament prophecies and demonstrate their fulfillment

in a myriad of ways. The most basic evidence of Jesus's deity is that both he and the New Testament writers asserted that he was divine. Claims of deity are probably the easiest to contrive, but they are still very important. After all, if neither Jesus nor the apostles ever claimed that Jesus was divine, we would have to wonder whether believing that Jesus is God is very important. Fortunately, there are more than enough references to Jesus's divine status to warrant our belief in this biblical doctrine. Space does not permit me to cover all of the references to Jesus's deity, but here is a representative sample.

Jesus's favorite way to refer to himself in Scripture is by the name "Son of Man." We see these references all through the Gospels (see, for example, Matt 8:20; Mark 2:28; Luke 5:24; and John 1:51). Jesus's use of this name is interesting because he appears to be referring back to the Old Testament prophets Ezekiel and Daniel. The Lord repeatedly called Ezekiel "son of man" when he was addressing him (see, for example, Ezek 2–4). It speaks to Ezekiel's calling as a prophet but also to his humble status.

Daniel, on the other hand, in a vision, saw "one like a son of man" (Dan 7:13). To that "son of man" was given "dominion, and glory, and a kingdom; so that those of every people, nation, and language should serve him. His dominion is an everlasting dominion that will not pass away, and his kingdom is one that will not be destroyed" (v. 14). Surely this was no humble prophet that Daniel saw in his vision. So when Jesus used "Son of Man" to refer to himself, was it the humble prophet of Ezekiel or the awesome eschatological figure of Daniel he had in mind? My guess is both. Certainly Jesus's use of "Son of Man" in Matt 19:28; 24:30; and 24:44 (see also Acts 7:56) had the Daniel references in mind. In those passages (and others like them), Jesus was predicting that he will return in glory and judgment—and those are God-like things to do.

Jesus announced that he was around in the time of Abraham (John 8:54–59). This is an interesting passage because the Pharisees' response makes clear what Jesus meant. Jesus told them that he preexisted even Abraham as the Son of God. (He even provocatively used the "I am" formula to identify himself in 8:58, which was famously used by the Lord to Moses in Exod 3:14.) That they understood this to be a claim to deity is evidenced by the fact that they picked up stones to kill him. (The temple was still under construction during Jesus's life so I imagine there was always plenty of such ammunition lying around.) Blasphemy was punishable by death in Jewish law (see Lev 24:16). The Pharisees were not going to execute him for the crime of saying confusing or cryptic things. They were going to kill him because he very clearly claimed to be God.

Other places where it was either insinuated or boldly claimed that Jesus is divine are John 1:1–4 (Jesus, before his birth, existed as one with God, was God, and created all things—much more on this passage later); John 5:19–29 (Jesus claimed the authority of end-times judgment and the power to raise the dead on the last day was his); and John 17:5 (Jesus claimed to exist in glory with God the Father before creation).

Remember "doubting" Thomas? He was skeptical that the reports of Jesus's resurrection were true and wanted to see it with his own eyes before he believed such a thing. When confronted by the "I-did-in-fact-rise-from-the-dead" Jesus, he cried out, "My Lord and my God!" (John 20:28). I sincerely doubt that Thomas was cursing, shocked by the sight of Jesus. Since Jesus did not rebuke him (see Jesus's response in 20:29), I think it is more likely that Jesus understood his exclamation to be a statement of faith, the proper recognition that the resurrected Jesus who stood before Thomas was none other than the Lord and God of life.

It is clear from the rest of the New Testament that Jesus's followers understood that Jesus was much more than a mere human. The apostle Paul, probably quoting a very early Christian hymn, taught that before his birth, Jesus existed "in the form of God" and "did not consider equality with God as something to be exploited" (that is, the Son did not grasp or hold on to equality with or being God for his own advantage — Phil 2:5–6). To the church in Corinth, Paul taught that the Lord who sustained and protected the Israelites as they left slavery in Egypt was none other than Christ (1 Cor 10:1–4). Jude echoed this by teaching that it was Jesus who saved the Israelites and destroyed the Egyptians in judgment (Jude 5). The author of Hebrews claimed that Jesus was the Creator and heir of all things (1:2); is "the radiance of God's glory and the exact expression of his nature, sustaining all things by his powerful word" (1:3); and then flat out called him "God" in 1:8. All that in just the first chapter of Hebrews! James, the half brother of Jesus, called him "our glorious Lord" and the one we must hold on to in faith (Jas 2:1). Peter wrote that Jesus was the preexistent one, "foreknown before the foundation of the world" but only revealed "in these last times" (1 Pet 1:20). In other words, every New Testament author taught and encouraged the church to see Jesus as divine, worthy of worship and faith.

Jesus Did Things Only God Can Do. To me, the most convincing and compelling demonstrations of the deity of Christ are not the explicit statements, but the fact that Jesus did things that rightly and properly only God can do. And I am not talking about the miracles here. Multiplying the loaves and fish to feed the multitudes, healing disease, opening blind eyes, even raising the dead are all amazing signs that serve, among other things, to demonstrate that Jesus was who he said he was. But they are not simple proof that Jesus is God. After all, the Old Testament prophets and new covenant apostles did all of those things, and they did them without being divine. But there are some things, beyond the miraculous, that God, and God alone, can do.

Creation is one of them. It is crystal clear from the very first verse of the Bible that "in the beginning" there was God and nothing else until God decided to create something else (Gen 1:1). So it is pretty impressive when the New Testament writers tell us things about Jesus like, "For everything was created by him, in heaven and on earth," and "all things have been created through him and for him" (Col 1:16). We will spend more time looking at this Colossians passage when we get to the "Thor heresy," but for now, you need to understand that no mere man was around or even had the smallest capacity to create the cosmos with God. There was only one Being doing the creating, and it wasn't a remarkable man—even the most remarkable of men. To be there "in the beginning," involved in creation, meant that you were God. And the biblical writers, such as Paul and John, did not even blush as they claimed that the Son of God was there, actively involved in the creation of the universe. "Oh, yeah. He was there—more than that, everything that was made was made *by* him and *for* him." To create the cosmos, one has to be God.

To me, though, the most persuasive argument that Jesus is divine comes from things that he did when he walked the earth—things that only God can do. Jesus forgave sin and accepted worship. And he did these things without the slightest hint of embarrassment or duplicity. This not only proves that Jesus is God, but it also proves that Jesus *knew* he was God.

There is a fantastic account in Mark 2:1–12 of Jesus teaching in the Galilean town of Capernaum, a town that would become his base of operations until his death and resurrection. There was such excitement about Jesus and his preaching on the kingdom that he attracted a crowd wherever he went, even when he was just hanging out at home. On one of these occasions, Jesus was there, "speaking the word" to a crowd that filled the room and spilled outside the door. Those who arrived late were out of luck—unless they made their own luck. Which is exactly what four enterprising men did for their paralyzed friend. The mass of people was so great that there was no hope of carrying their buddy into the room through the door, so they decided to create a door *in the ceiling*. Obviously, these men were pinning all of their hopes for their friend on Jesus.

Imagine what it would have been like to be there. Jesus was teaching on the kingdom to a packed house (literally), a little debris began to fall from the ceiling, and suddenly, a man was lowered in front of Jesus. How would he react? What would he say? As usual, Jesus did not disappoint. He told the paralyzed man, "Son, your sins are forgiven."

In the crowd were some scribes—these were basically religious lawyers, experts in the law. They said to themselves what anybody in the room who had his theology straight was thinking. "Why does he speak like this? He's blaspheming! Who can forgive sins but God alone?" The scribes were right. Unless the paralyzed man had actually wronged Jesus in some way, Jesus had no right to forgive him. Now, unless I hold a position of legal authority, like a judge, I can only forgive someone who sins against me. I have no authority to forgive someone for a sin committed against someone else. There is no reason to think that the paralyzed man had ever met Jesus, let alone wronged him. Unless of course Jesus is God. Only God is sinned against every time somebody does something wrong, and only God has the legal authority to act as Judge of the cosmos. So only God has the ultimate authority, both personally and legally, to forgive someone his sins.

The scribes understood this perfectly. When Jesus told the man his sins were forgiven, the scribes did not take his statement to be one of sentimental compassion. They understood that he was claiming something for himself that only God by rights could do. Hence Jesus's response. "Fine—talk is cheap, I suppose. Which is easier: to say, 'Your sins are forgiven,' or to say, 'Get up and walk'? But so that you will know that I do have the authority to forgive sins . . ." Then Jesus turned to the paralyzed man and commanded him to rise, pick up his bed, and go home. And the man obeyed. He who could not walk just seconds earlier was miraculously healed.

I guess that one might dismiss Jesus's forgiving the man as self-delusional crazy talk and blasphemy. The scribes initially did. But then Jesus backed it up by healing a paralyzed man. This was not a man suffering from a bad back, the kind of malady that big-haired televangelists will "heal" someone of on television. This was a paralyzed man, no doubt well-known as such in the community, and Jesus healed him in front of a packed house. No self-delusional blasphemer could heal someone like that. His miracle backed up his claim. He did forgive that man's sins, and he did it because of the very logic of the scribes. He had the authority to forgive because he was and is God. And what is more, he knew it. No Batman-like Jesus could or would do this.

Jesus consciously did another thing that demonstrates his deity. He accepted worship. Remember that Jesus was and is Jewish. He obeyed and fulfilled the Jewish law perfectly (Matt 5:17). Jesus was a faithful monotheist and knew that the God of Abraham, Isaac, Jacob, and Moses was and is the only true God. Further, the one true God described himself as a jealous God, one who will not share his glory with anyone else, least of all a man (Exod 20:5; Isa 48:11). (Remember what happened to Herod in Acts 12:23–24 when he accepted the worship of God. The punishment involved agony, being eaten by worms, and death—not pleasant!) And yet there are numerous times throughout Jesus's life when he accepted the praise and worship of others. You could say that his life on earth was inaugurated with worship. The angels celebrated the birth of Christ in song (Luke 2:8–14), while the Magi, "falling to their knees" before the infant Lord, "worshiped him" (Matt 2:11).

Jesus, in fact, desired to be glorified. Comparing him to angels is helpful. Whenever an angel appeared to humans, the results were predictable. People would either express terror or want to fall down and worship—so majestic were the beings before them. The angels in turn always said some variation of the same thing—"Fear not" or "Get up." They of all beings knew who was to be worshiped (the Lord) and who was not (them). Jesus, though, did not even blink when people wanted to praise, glorify, or worship him (see Matt 14:33; 28:9; John 9:38). In fact, he even had the guts to ask the Lord to share his glory with him. An important focus in Jesus's prayer in the garden of Gethsemane, the most poignant prayer in all the Bible, uttered in the shadow of the cross, is the glory of Christ. In it, Jesus asked the Father to glorify him (John 17:2), restoring the glory he had enjoyed with the Father before the world existed (17:5). He claimed that he was glorified in the ones his Father had given him (17:10), and his most fervent prayer for his followers was that they might be with him, so that they would see the glory that the Father had given him (17:24). What kind of mere man prays to God the Father, asking him to share his divine glory with him?

We have already seen Thomas's reaction to the risen Christ, but that pales in comparison to the vision that John had.

In Revelation 4, the curtain is drawn back on heaven and John is given a view of the very throne room of God. The rest of chapter 4 describes what John saw, and it is awesome. John was asked to write what he saw, and you get the feeling he is hanging on by his fingernails as he tries to describe the breathtaking

sight before him. He grasps for words, and language fails him
as he resorts to metaphors and similes. ("[It] was like . . . [It]
had the appearance of . . .") He describes the throne and its sur-
roundings, barely even trying to describe the one seated on the
throne. There are all these incredible beings: twenty-four elders,
each on a throne and wearing a crown, and four amazing and
strange "living creatures," each covered with eyes. If you ask
me who these folk are, I will give you the three most important
words in theology: *I don't know*. I couldn't tell you. But what
I do know is that they are wondrous and they are engaged in
perfect continuous worship of the one God, praising him for his
eternality, holiness, worthiness, and for being the Creator of all
things. Everything in heaven is exactly as it should be. God is on
his throne, surrounded by beings created to worship, and it is
awesome (in the absolute truest sense of the word—if anything
has ever warranted being called "awesome" it is this).

Everything is as it should be—that is, until a scroll is brought
in (Rev 5:1). We are not told immediately what the scroll is, but
we later find that it is God's plan to set everything right in the
cosmos, to bring justice and restoration to the broken world,
to finally vindicate the righteous and punish the wicked. It is
God's plan to finally, once and for all, balance the scales of justice. Written on that scroll is the Lord's definitive, satisfying
answer to anyone who has ever cried, "How long, O Lord?" It
is God's powerful and perfect response to all the suffering and
agony that is part of this present dark world. And we are told
that the seals on the scroll cannot be broken, the plan cannot be
executed, justice cannot prevail, because there is no one, anywhere, who is worthy to do so. It is not for lack of applicants or
a thorough search. Anyone, anywhere, who is alive or has ever
been alive is considered and then rejected (5:3). No one is even
worthy to look into it. No one. And John breaks. It is too much
for him. Confronted with the absolute glory of God and then

the prospect of the failure of justice, he falls into despair and begins to wail (5:4).

But then an elder steps forward and tells John, "Do not weep." A worthy one has finally been found. He is the Lion of the tribe of Judah (the one prophesied by Jacob way back in Genesis 49). He is the Root of David (the one prophesied in 2 Samuel 7, where Nathan told David that he would one day have an heir whose destiny is to inhabit an eternal throne). Now, I know of only one person whom the biblical writers believe fits that description—Jesus! He is the one worthy because he "has conquered" (Rev 5:5). And in one of the coolest moments in all of literature, John turns to look at this conquering, regal Lion and sees . . . *a Lamb*! And not just any old lamb, but one "like a slaughtered lamb," but who also possesses power and wisdom and the Spirit of God (5:6). We are later told that the Lamb conquered through being slain and rising as a ransom for the people of God (5:9–12). If there was ever any doubt that it is Jesus, it should be removed now. The Lamb walked to the throne and took the scroll out of the strong right hand of God (5:7).

At that point, something remarkable happened. All those creatures who had been praising God on this throne, those very beings who had been designed and made to offer perfect worship, turned and fell down in worship "before the Lamb" (5:8). And they did this in the very presence of God the Father seated on his throne! Now, I have to ask, if there were ever any beings who had their theology straight, who understood what worship is and the penalty and implications of worshiping the wrong being, don't you think it would be these folks? And if they made a mistake and were not supposed to worship the Lamb, given their proximity to God himself, don't you think there would have been some swift and terrible correction? (Again, recall what happened to Herod in Acts 12:23–24 when he accepted the worship owed to God.) I suppose that God can be long-suffering with his fallen creatures on earth who engage in bogus worship, *but not in his own throne room*! And yet that correction does not come. I am left with only one conclusion. The God who will not share his glory with another is quite willing to share his glory with Jesus because in some remarkable and robust way, Jesus must himself be the one true God. A Batman-like Jesus will not work in this passage. And that, in my estimation, is the strongest demonstration of the deity of Jesus Christ in all of the Bible.

Why Is This Important?

So the Bible says that Jesus is divine. Why is that important? Why is it necessary that we believe that Jesus is divine? I mean, why is someone like Batman, the most remarkable of humans, but only a human, not good enough? What if Jesus were just a man, but a man who was the wisest, the most brilliant, the most compassionate, the most gifted teacher, and the most charismatic leader? What if God did amazing miracles through him, more so even than Elijah or Moses? Wouldn't such a man have been good enough? Well, it depends on the question, "Good enough for what?" Good enough to inspire people and correct some faulty thinking? Good enough to heal some folk and provide an incredible example that will motivate people for millennia? Sure. Absolutely. But good enough to reconcile people to God? Good enough to usher in the promised kingdom of God? No. Not even close. The gospel will not work and its blessings cannot come if Jesus is just a man, even the most remarkable of men. In other words, we need Jesus to be more than Batman. And here is why.

Salvation Belongs to the Lord. One of the more incredible stories in the Bible is found in the book of Jonah. This reluctant

prophet had been tossed into the sea while trying to run away
from the task the Lord had given him. Death by drowning was
his certain destiny. But the Lord intervened on Jonah's behalf,
sending a great fish, which swallowed Jonah and transported
him to dry land. The undersea voyage took some time (three
days and three nights), giving Jonah plenty of opportunity to
reflect on what had just happened. Jonah prayed to the Lord,
recounting the event that had almost killed him, and concluded
his prayer with the great statement, "Salvation belongs to the
Lord" (Jonah 2:9).

Jonah spoke better than he knew. And if you won't take a
reluctant prophet's word, how about that of God himself: "I—I
am the Lord. Besides me, there is no Savior" (Isa 43:11).

God is not just the best at rescuing people from drowning.
He is able to rescue us from our deepest dangers and calamities,
including our broken relationship with God and certain con-
demnation because of it. We humans have made such a mess of
things that the only one who can save us is God. We have fallen
and we cannot get up. In fact, we can't even cry out for help, so
pathetic is our predicament. We saw in the last chapter that sin
and the curse were caused by humans and therefore required a
human solution. The rub is that humanity was and is absolutely
and fundamentally unable to save itself. If any saving is to be
done, it has to be initiated and carried out by God. The Bible
describes us as "dead" in trespasses and sins (Eph 2:1). And this
is not a "mostly dead" situation from which Miracle Max can
save us. We are "really most sincerely dead," unable and even
unwilling to save ourselves. To make matters worse, we have
alienated ourselves from the only one who can save us, becoming "by nature children under wrath" (Eph 2:3). Jesus had to be
human in order to atone for human sin. But if he were actually
and completely to save us, Jesus had to be divine as well. It is
axiomatic—salvation belongs to the Lord.

Jesus's Blood Is Precious. It takes a human, but something more than a mere human to save humanity, at least the kind of salvation that the Bible talks about. But the blood of Jesus, who is fully human and fully divine, is able to do so. Now, the Bible does not say it like that in so many words, but I think that 1 Pet 1:18–21 teaches this concept. Peter explained that our salvation has been bought for us, not by things that we normally associate with being costly, things like gold and silver, but by something far more precious—the blood of Christ. He likened Christ to an "unblemished and spotless lamb," clearly teaching that Jesus was a perfect atoning sacrifice. The description points to the sinlessness of Christ in his humanity. But then Peter referenced Jesus as the one "foreknown before the foundation of the world" (1:20). "Foreknown" suggests far more than mere cognition on the part of God, as though God merely knew, like a fortune-teller, what was going to happen. His being foreknown by God means that God intimately knew and was committed to Christ, and this before the world was even an idea. Christ was later "revealed" in the "last times" for us. He was revealed, not created. Then, because of his great work, God did something that he never does to anyone else. He "gave him glory" (1:21). As we just saw, that means that Christ is God.

With what were we ransomed? The blood of Christ, which is really just another way of saying the life of Christ. How precious is the life of Christ? His is no ordinary human life. It is not even the life of an extraordinary, but mere, human. It is the life of God-become-man. This incredible being, Jesus Christ, gave his life for us. And that life was sufficient to save us.

The Lord's Salvation Is Bigger than Just You and Me. The gospel is the good news of God's saving work in Jesus Christ. It is the message of the work of God in Christ that saves all those who put their faith in Christ. But the work of Christ is much bigger than making sure you and I get to go to heaven when we die. No, the Lord had bigger goals than that. Jesus Christ reconciled *all things* to God. Look at Col 1:15–20. We are told that Jesus is "the image of the invisible God" (1:15). Whereas before, no one had ever seen God, there is such continuity of character and essence between Jesus and God that to see Jesus was to see God (see John 14:9). He is the one by whom, through whom, and for whom all things were created (1:16). This is more God-talk, not the description of an extraordinary, but mere human. In 1:19, Paul claims that "God was pleased to have all his fullness dwell in him." That Greek word translated "all" means ALL. (It is a really good translation.) Everything essential that makes God who he is, was (and is) incarnate in Jesus. So it should come as no surprise that Jesus was able to reconcile "everything [same word translated "all" in the previous verse] to himself, whether things on earth or things in heaven, by making peace through his blood, shed on the cross" (1:20). Jesus can do that because he is divine. It would take God to accomplish such a great salvation, because, after all, salvation belongs to the Lord. And when all is said and done, Jesus will rule over all of the cosmos—everything in heaven and on earth. He will rule over it all as a human, the promised Davidic heir, but he will also rule over it as the one who both created and redeemed it—the King of kings and Lord of lords. A mere human, even the most remarkable of mere humans (like Batman), could never do that. But Jesus can, because he is wonderfully so much more than merely human.

Batman cannot save you. But Jesus, who is God in the flesh, can.

Discussion Questions

Questions for Personal Reflection

- How does the deity of Jesus inspire your worship of Jesus?
- How does the deity of Jesus inspire your commitment and witness to Jesus?
- Do you ever doubt that Jesus is truly and fully God? If so, what might give you confidence?

Questions for Group Discussion

- Describe a time when you were tempted to minimize or deny the deity of Jesus. What was motivating you or inhibiting you?
- Why will the gospel not work if Jesus is not truly and fully God?
- What are some implications of the fact that Jesus can forgive all sin? How might that change the way you pray and live?
- What are some implications of the fact that the angels in heaven worship Jesus Christ? How might that change the way you worship and live?

For Further Study

Read Matt 14:22–36. Consider the response of Jesus's disciples in verse 33. Was their response of worship and statement correct? If so, how might this encourage your devotion and commitment to Jesus?

3

ANT-MAN CAN'T SAVE YOU

THE MENACE OF MODALISM	JESUS WAS ONE OF THREE "COSTUMES" OF THE ONE GOD

For me, Ant-Man wasn't enough, now I'm Giant-Man. I figure if that doesn't make me tough enough, someday I'll invent another persona.
—Hank Pym as Giant-Man, *Avengers* 1, no. 3 (January 1964)

Jesus Christ is the same yesterday, today, and forever.
—Hebrews 13:8

As a child, I was remarkably short, all through junior high and well into high school. And when I say short, I am not talking just a little below average. I am talking shortest-person-in-the-class-every-year short. Not just the shortest boy; I was the shortest person, often shorter than everyone a grade below me. Occasionally an elementary school teacher would have my class line up by height for who knows what reason, and I still remember that sinking feeling of dread as I hopelessly walked to the end of the line, praying that I might quickly grow a few inches before I took my place in shrimp purgatory. Those quick prayers of desperation were never answered to my satisfaction. Being vertically challenged was no fun.

I wanted no part of being small. So, when one of my friends told me about the Atom, a DC superhero who could shrink down to subatomic size, I was less than impressed. After a lifetime of being short, I could see no advantage to such a "power." A superhero who could shrink even smaller than I already was? No thanks. I knew there was nothing super or heroic about being small.

I didn't buy any Atom comics.

I eventually grew a little bit. Perhaps my new height gave me a better vantage point from which to survey the possibilities of superheroes who can shrink. And though the Atom never captured my imagination, Ant-Man, the diminutive Marvel superhero, has grown large in my esteem. But he can do far more than just go small.

The original Ant-Man is the alter ego of Dr. Henry "Hank" Pym, a biophysicist and security operations expert. Pym discovered a chemical substance that he eventually called "Pym Particles." These particles, properly utilized, allow the user to alter his size. Pym developed a suit that enabled him to harness the particles and shrink to the size of an insect. This was a lot of fun until he got stuck in an anthill, where he survived only because a friendly ant rescued him. (A superhero that owes his life to a merciful ant? Not an auspicious beginning . . .) Despite the humbling experience, Pym became convinced that he should communicate with ants, because if you are going to be the size of an ant, you had best be on good terms with them for the sake of self-preservation. He was able to invent a cybernetic helmet whereby he could communicate with ants and other insects through the transmission of psionic/pheromonal/electrical waves. The suit also enabled Pym to maintain his normal human strength even when shrunk to the size of an ant. This creates a relative superpower, as normal human strength delivered by an ant-size person packs a phenomenal high-pressure punch.

As cool as it might be to shrink to the size of an insect, the power to go small is not always the most helpful (as I well knew from my own experience). Fortunately, Hank Pym discovered that the Pym Particles worked the other way as well. They could also be used to go big, and I mean really big. Twelve-feet big. When Pym went large, he assumed the name "Giant-Man." (Not terribly clever, but his brain cells were apparently too busy developing Pym Particles to come up with a cool nickname.) Later, Pym changed the Giant-Man moniker to "Goliath" (still not terribly clever), but eventually went back to the Giant-Man identity. Same powers, same man; different costume and different name. Ant-Man and Giant-Man were so phenomenal that Hank Pym was one of the founding members of the Avengers.

A significant limitation of the suit was that when Hank Pym was Ant-Man, he could not be Giant-Man. When he was really small, he was not simultaneously really big. And when he was Giant-man, he was not Ant-man. Pym had to be one or the other. Ant-Man and Giant-Man were never fighting crime simultaneously. The reason is obvious. There is one Hank Pym, and Ant-Man and Giant-Man were personas or modes of the one person, Hank Pym. When Pym was fighting crime, anyone hoping for help from both Ant-Man and Giant-Man was out of luck. You got one or the other, but never both at the same time.

Later, Pym had an emotional breakdown (being the size of an ant will do that to a guy) and added some wings and yellow color to his Ant-Man costume and became "Yellowjacket."[1] This

---

[1] In the 2015 movie adaptation, *Ant-Man*, Yellowjacket is the arch-enemy of Hank Pym and Scott Lang (Pym's hand-selected replacement). But in the Marvel comics, Yellowjacket was an alter-ego of Pym.

manifestation of Pym was a bit on the cocky side and suffered from a kind of schizophrenia (the kind where you claim to have killed Hank Pym—your true identity—and are generally disliked, distrusted, and considered unsafe by everyone you meet).

So, if you are keeping track, Hank Pym now has three identities or modes of being. And just as with Ant-Man and Giant-Man, when Pym was Yellowjacket, neither Ant-Man nor Giant-Man was anywhere to be found. The one person Pym had three different options, but he could not be all three at the same time in the same place. When Yellowjacket was around, Ant-Man was not (no matter how much people would have liked a trade). The three personae or modes were not present simultaneously. Pym had to pick and choose which mode to take, which costume to wear, which set of superpowers to employ.

Now, all of this is probably not surprising in the least. That is just the way things work. After all, Hank Pym was one guy with three different costumes. There were not really three different persons who could coexist. There was only one person, who could take on three different roles, but never all at the same time. You would be right to ask, "So what? What's the big deal?" And I would respond, "You are right. It's no big deal—if we are talking about Hank Pym."

But if we are talking about God, it is a really big deal, because it is a really big error.

There are many, throughout history all the way to today, who feel that God is kind of like Hank Pym, with his different costumes and modes. Sometimes God decides to be the Father. Sometimes he becomes the Son. And sometimes he is the Spirit. But since God is one being, he cannot be the Father and the Son and the Spirit at the same time. He has to pick one and only one at any one time. The three different "modes" do not coexist simultaneously. Such thinking is easy to understand, but it is dead wrong.

I call the belief that Jesus Christ was just one of three possible modes of God, or costumes worn by God, the "Ant-Man heresy." It is more commonly called *modalism* or *Sabellianism*, and it has been around for a long time. As we will find out, Jesus-as-a-mode-of-God might be easy to understand, but "Ant-Man Jesus" cannot save you.

THE HERESY

Let's face it, the Christian doctrine of the Trinity is hard to understand.

That is not to say that the Bible is unclear in the things that it affirms.[2] On the contrary, the Bible, in straightforward manner, teaches the main points of the Trinity. The Christian doctrine of the Trinity is based on five biblical affirmations being true.

Affirmation 1: There is only one God. Though there might be rivals and pretenders to the throne, Scripture is adamant that there is only one ultimate Creator God. Take, for example, Isa 45:5: "I am the LORD, and there is no other, there is no God but me." The apostle Paul is equally adamant: "We know that 'an idol is nothing in the world,' and that 'there is no God but one'" (1 Cor 8:4). From the start to the finish of the Bible, the testimony is clear; there is only one God.

Affirmation 2: The Father is God. The one Creator God of the Old Testament is usually identified as God the Father, the one written of in the New Testament. Jesus referred to God as his Father all through the Sermon on the Mount (Matthew 5–7) and the Gospel of John, while the New Testament authors

---

[2] The word *Trinity* does not appear in the Bible. It is a word that Christian theologians have used ever since Tertullian coined the term in the second century to describe what the Bible teaches on the triune nature of God.

routinely refer to God the Father in their letters (e.g., Rom 1:7; Gal 1:1; Heb 2:11; Jas 1:27; 1 Pet 1:17; etc.).

Affirmation 3: The Son is God. We looked at the biblical evidence for the deity of Jesus Christ in chapter 2. There was a lot of it. (See John 1:1–4; 5:19–29; 17:5; Phil 2:5–6; Heb 1:2–3; Rev 5).

Affirmation 4: The Holy Spirit is God. The New Testament also teaches that the Holy Spirit is God in a way that cannot be reduced to the Spirit being the presence or power of the one God. The Spirit makes God-like decisions, like who gets what spiritual gifts (1 Cor 12:11) and which missionaries should go where (Acts 13:2). The Spirit is also identified as God in the sad affair of Ananias and Sapphira when Ananias's lying to the Spirit is equated with lying to God (Acts 5:3–4).

Affirmation 5: The Father is not the Son is not the Spirit. There are places in the Bible where two or three members of the Trinity are working simultaneously, so it cannot be that the Father is the same person as the Son or the Spirit—they are distinct. Consider Jesus's baptism, where the Son comes out of the water, the Spirit descends upon the Son, and the Father speaks from heaven (Matt 3:13–17). We will dig into this deeper in a moment, but for now it seems that the Father, Son, and Holy Spirit cannot be the same person because they are all at the baptism together.

The Bible is very clear in affirming those five things. The problem lies in how it can be that all five affirmations are true at the same time. It is interesting that in the early church one option that was never taken was to deny that there was only one God. The Old Testament teaches monotheism, and so did Jesus, so moving to a "three Gods" idea was never seriously entertained. So the question remained, how can there be only one God and yet the Father, Son, and Holy Spirit are God at the same time?

During the second and third centuries, the church struggled to make sense of these teachings, and one idea that was proposed was to deny the fifth affirmation. A priest and theologian named Sabellius, who lived at the turn of the third century (late 100s and early 200s), proposed that the Father, Son, and Holy Spirit were not separate persons per se, but were just hats or costumes that the one God wears at specific times. So according to Sabellius, there are not three or even two coexistent divine persons or beings. Rather, there is only one God, only one person, who plays three different roles at different times in human history.

Sabellius even divided up the roles of God according to specific eras. All the time covered in the Old Testament was the era of the role of God the Father. The time covered in the Gospels was the era of the role of Jesus the Son. And the present time, from the ascension of Jesus until today, is the era of the role of the Spirit. So, according to Sabellius, God is rather like Hank Pym, choosing from one of three roles or modes depending on the need and the time.

Sabellius's solution of "Ant-Man Jesus" has the advantage of being easy to understand. There is one God who assumes different roles at different times. The proposal is easy to comprehend. The problem is that it is not at all biblical. In fact, there are some biblical teachings, as we will see, that flatly deny Sabellius's proposal.[3]

---

[3] Not much else is known about Sabellius. His homeland was most likely Libya, but it appears that he did most of his teaching in Rome. We do know that he was excommunicated for his ideas by Callistus, the bishop of Rome, in AD 220. We have no extant (existing) copies of any of his writings, as they were all destroyed. But his bad idea about Jesus and the Trinity was named after him—Sabellianism. Which only goes to show, if you want to make a name for yourself in the annals of church history, the easiest route is to make up a really bad idea about Jesus and start promoting it. I would never recommend that path, however, because it will probably cost you your soul.

WHO COMMITS THE
ANT-MAN HERESY TODAY?

As I said earlier, the Christian doctrine of the Trinity is that the one God exists simultaneously as three coeternal and coequal persons: the Father, the Son, and the Holy Spirit. This does not imply that there are three Gods. There are three persons in the one God. Nor does it imply that the one God is divided up into three equal parts, each of whom is one-third God. No, everything that it takes to be God the Father, God the Son, and God the Holy Spirit, each possesses completely. Think of it this way: if there were an exhaustive checklist of God attributes and prerogatives, covering everything that it takes to be completely divine, the Father, Son, and Holy Spirit would each be able to individually check every box.

There is no doubt that the Trinity is difficult to understand. It can be tough sledding to try and explain how there can be only one God and yet the Father, Son, and Holy Spirit can each exist completely as God at the same time. We should expect such difficulty when, as finite creatures, we try to describe our infinite Creator God. But tough sledding does not mean that it is impossible, and it certainly does not give us the right to make something up that appears to work but actually contradicts the Bible.

The most prominent adherents to the Ant-Man heresy are found in the so-called Jesus only/Oneness Pentecostal movement. Oneness Pentecostals (found, for example, in the United Pentecostal Church International) are convinced that there is only one God, but that the one God does not exist in three separate and simultaneous persons. Rather, the Son is the Father is the Spirit. The God who created (the Father) is the same God who died for us (taking the form of the Son) *and* the same God who regenerates believers and leads them day to day (in the form of the Spirit). Of course, what Oneness Pentecostals believe is just good-old fashioned modalism, the kind that would make Sabellius proud. Or to put it another way, to the Oneness Pentecostal, God is, again, much like Hank Pym, who must choose between being Ant-Man or Giant-Man or Yellowjacket at any one time, but can never be all three or even two of them simultaneously. Likewise, God can choose between being the Father or the Son or the Holy Spirit. They are just different costumes or roles, and they do not coexist at the same time.

In my experience, the Ant-Man heresy is the most widespread of all the bad ideas about Jesus and the Trinity in the church. (Who knew that Ant-Man could be so popular?) Now, most people that I know would never consciously self-identify as a follower of Sabellius, modalism, or even the Ant-Man heresy. But that does not mean that people do not unwittingly hold the position. And it can happen without our even noticing it. Here is what I mean:

A popular teaching illustration is to liken the Trinity to water. It is explained that there is one substance, water, but it can exist in three different states: liquid, vapor, and solid (ice). The problem is that water is either liquid, vapor, or ice. It is not all three at the same time.

All you high school scientific types are probably thinking, *What about the triple point of water, where all three states can theoretically coexist at a temperature of 273.16 degrees Kelvin and a pressure of 611.73 pascals?* Well, good luck finding those conditions anywhere but in a lab! (And if you were in my high school labs, you were never able to get the experiment to work, so I am kind of a skeptic. Just saying . . .) But even if you were one of the chosen few who could make the high school lab vacuum apparatus work, you have to recognize that any one molecule of H_2O (that is the molecular formula for water, for all you non-high school scientific types) can exist only as vapor or liquid or solid, even at the so-called triple point. So we are back to modalism. The illustration breaks down pretty quickly and is probably a better teaching tool for the Ant-Man heresy than for what God is actually like. It explains how Hank Pym can be Ant-Man, but it does not explain how Jesus is God.

I have been in Bible studies where the question of the Trinity comes up and people just throw their hands in the air and say, "It's too complicated for me. I just like to think of God being either the Father, the Son, or the Holy Spirit at any one time, and it keeps me from getting a headache." Well, no one wants a headache, but what we believe and know matters. If you would rather be wrong than have to engage in some deep thinking, you might want to reconsider your strategy. It is dishonest and it dishonors the Lord to remake him into someone that is easier for us to understand. Take an Advil and plunge into the Bible!

Any time you confuse the roles in the Trinity, you have fallen into the Ant-Man error. One common occurrence is in Lord's Supper meditations and prayers. I don't know how many times I have heard someone address a prayer to God the Father and eventually thank him (God the Father) for dying on the cross. The problem is that it was Jesus, the Son of God, not God the Father, who was crucified. I suspect that anyone who is asked to pray before Communion knows that it was God the Son, not God the Father, who died on the cross. Yet through carelessness or neglect, the mistake is made. And the mistake has a name: The belief that God the Father suffered and died on the cross is called *Patripassianism* (or, if you like, a kind of Ant-Man heresy), and the church condemned such thinking long ago. And for good reason: as we will discover later in this chapter, Patripassianism destroys the very logic of the gospel.

What we think about God matters. We have not been told all the ins and outs of the Trinity, all that the three persons do, nor have we been given an exhaustive guide to how they relate. But we have been told some things, and like all of God's revelation to us, what he has told us is for our good (check out Deut 29:29). So we would do well to pay close attention to what the Bible says about each member of the Trinity and what each of them does. Then we can be intentional in our thoughts and words to and about God.

WHAT THE BIBLE SAYS

The New Testament teaches that God the Father, God the Son, and God the Holy Spirit are three different persons who exist simultaneously and interact with one another. Any time the Bible records an event where two or three members of the Trinity are interacting, we have a pretty strong case against the Ant-Man heresy. Let's look at some of the evidence.

Early in Jesus's public ministry, he went to John the Baptist to be baptized. The story is recorded in Matt 3:13–17. There are lots of questions surrounding why Jesus went to John, because John offered a baptism of repentance symbolizing the individual's need for and readiness for the coming messianic kingdom (see vv. 5–12). Jesus did not need to repent of anything, nor did he need to ready himself for the coming kingdom in the same manner that everyone else did. Jesus came as the King of the kingdom of God, not its subject. In fact, John's baptism in water was meant to prepare God's people for the greater baptism of the Spirit that Jesus himself would bring (vv. 11–12).

Our questions as to why Jesus wanted to be baptized are completely legitimate because John himself asked the question: "I need to be baptized by you, and yet you come to me?" (v. 14). And let's face it, Jesus's response, "Allow it for now, because this is the way for us to fulfill all righteousness," is a bit on the cryptic side (v. 15). If the one named "John the Baptist" could not figure out why Jesus was standing in front of him in the water, then I think our questions are OK.

By my way of thinking, Jesus went to John to be baptized to associate himself with John's ministry. John was commissioned by the Lord to prepare God's people for the coming Messiah. He was the prophet predicted back in Old Testament times, another Elijah, who would announce the arrival of the long-awaited day of the Lord (Mal 4:5; Matt 11:14). In God's plan, the forerunner to the Messiah would, of course, precede the Messiah. John was that man. He was a magnetic preacher, living like Elijah, the strange prophet of old, who asked people to come, not to the temple city of Jerusalem to get ready, but to the wilderness outside the city. The missions of John and Jesus were inextricably linked. John was appointed by God to prepare people for Jesus and to point him out when he arrived. So I think that Jesus went to John to be baptized in order to validate John's ministry. It was Jesus's way of telling everybody that John was a legit prophet, and that he and John were together a part of God's master plan to finally make all things right.

So John baptized Jesus. Although he was probably a bit nervous, he did what he had done hundreds of times when he was standing in the Jordan River with someone hoping to receive baptism. But what happened next was unlike any of the previous baptisms.

Matthew tells us that as Jesus came out of the water, the "heavens suddenly opened." I have no idea what this means, but it must have been awesome. Clearly, this was not your garden-variety baptism. And out of the heavens "the Spirit of God descended like a dove" and landed on Jesus (3:16). Earlier, the Lord had told John to look out for the person upon whom the Spirit would descend and remain. That person would be the Son of God and the one who would baptize with the Spirit (John 1:32–34). So John understood that when the Spirit descended and landed on Jesus, he might actually be standing in the presence of the Son of God himself.

If John was even a little unsure, those doubts were quickly removed by what happened next. A voice boomed from heaven: "This is my beloved Son, with whom I am well-pleased" (Matt 3:17). My translation: "This is my Son. He makes me happy!" Imagine being John. The long-awaited Messiah came to him to be baptized, and then the next thing he knew, God the Father and God the Spirit joined the party. The triple point of the Trinity, all three members were right there at the same exact time, and John had a front-row seat.

So we should pause and ask, "If God is like Ant-Man, wearing different costumes or assuming different personae at different times, how can we account for what we just read about Jesus's baptism?"

The answer is, we can't. It is as simple as that.

If the Father and the Son and the Holy Spirit are just personae that the one God assumes at any one time, then they cannot coexist simultaneously, and the account of Jesus's baptism is impossible. Now, I suppose that Jesus could have summoned a dove to descend and thrown his voice to make people believe that God the Father had spoken. But that would require a very strange (and cynical) reading of the story. I mean, who knew that Jesus was a dove-whispering, quick-change artist and ventriloquist? You have to be pretty committed to the Ant-Man heresy to read the Bible like that. A much easier (and faithful) reading is to understand that Jesus and the Father and the Spirit were there *at the same time* because they are three different and simultaneously existing persons.

Another obvious example of the simultaneous existence of different persons of the Trinity is when Jesus prayed. Matthew 26:36–42 records the account of Jesus's final moments of freedom in the garden of Gethsemane before his arrest, hours that he spent in prayer. Jesus was clearly under extreme duress. This was no time for pretending—Jesus was about to die, and he knew it. The anxiety of what he was about to face came close to overwhelming him, and he cried out to the Lord to come up with a different way, if possible. If Jesus and the Father and the Spirit are three roles that the one God plays, then to whom was Jesus talking when he prayed? Was he talking to himself? People who talk to themselves at that level are delusional, have multiple personality disorder, are demon-possessed, or worse. None of those options is particularly desirable in the Savior of the world. Not even Hank Pym as Yellowjacket talked to himself like that!

I think the best way to read the account of Jesus praying in the garden of Gethsemane is to understand that when Jesus "began to be sorrowful and troubled," when he "fell facedown and prayed" (Matt 26:37, 39), he was in control of his faculties and addressed his prayer to the Father, whom he understood to be a different person from himself. In this case, it was God the Father, and talking to him is what made it prayer.

I mentioned earlier that it did not take a big church council to meet and condemn Sabellianism. All it really took was Christians reading their Bibles and asking some commonsense questions. The Ant-Man heresy just can't be true when we read Bible stories in which the Father and the Son are at the same place at the same time. God the Father, God the Son, and God the Holy Spirit can't be different personae in light of passages like this.

WHY IS THIS IMPORTANT?

What does it matter if you get the Trinity right? I mean, do you have to pass a theology test to relate rightly to God and get to heaven? I have given a lot of exams over the years, and I will be the first to admit that none of them carry that kind of penalty — separation from God — for failing.

But what we believe about Jesus and the Trinity is important because it has huge implications for how we understand the gospel and, thus, how we live. For example, do you realize that the very practice of Christian prayer is dependent upon God existing as Father, Son, and Holy Spirit? That is, if Jesus were like Ant-Man, then his instructions on how his followers are to pray would make no sense and would not work at all. Do you realize that the gospel requires all three members of the Trinity — Father, Son, and Holy Spirit — to be actively involved simultaneously every step of the way? And that if God is more like Hank Pym than he is the triune God revealed in the Bible, then the gospel disintegrates before our eyes? Here is why.

Ant-Man Cannot Answer Prayer. Prayer seems easy enough, doesn't it? Isn't it just talking to God? Why do we need three persons? What about people in the Old Testament who prayed to the Lord and their prayers were heard? They didn't understand the Trinity, so why should we? Let's let Jesus answer these questions.

At one point in Jesus's ministry, his disciples asked him to teach them how to pray. His response, beginning in Luke 11:2, is important: "Whenever you pray, say, 'Father, your name be honored as holy.'" To be clear, Jesus always addressed his own prayers to the Father (see Matt 11:25; 26:39–43, 53; Mark 14:36; Luke 10:21; John 12:27–28; 14:16; 17:1-25), and he instructed his disciples to do the same: pray to the Father (Matt 6:5–6, 9; 7:11; Luke 11:11–13; John 16:23–26). The examples of the prayers of the apostles and New Testament letter writers are all addressed to either the Lord or to the Father (see, for example, Eph 3:14–21; Col 1:3, 12; 3:17).

But Jesus said more than just, "pray to the Father." Indeed, Jesus thrust himself right into the middle of prayer by instructing his disciples to pray in *his* (Jesus's) name. He told all who follow him, when they go to the Father in prayer, to ask "in my name" (John 14:13; 15:16; 16:23, 24, 26). The disciples learned that lesson. In the book of Acts, the apostles seemed to do everything in Jesus's name (see, for example, Acts 2:38; 3:6; 9:27; 16:18). Paul prayed "in the name of our Lord Jesus Christ" (Eph 5:20). So Jesus's instruction is to pray to the Father in the name of the Son.

But Christian prayer is not limited to just the Father and the Son. Jesus promised in John 14–16 to send the Spirit, calling him the "Counselor" (or "Helper," "Advocate," or "Comforter," depending on the translation of the Greek word *paracletos*). According to Jesus, the Spirit would guide and teach his followers, remind them of his words, enable them to abide in him, bear witness through them, and declare the words of Jesus to and through them—basically everything essential to faithful Christian living. So it comes as no surprise that the apostle Paul would instruct Christians to pray "in the Spirit" (Eph 6:18). As a matter of fact, sometimes the Spirit will take matters into his own hands and pray for us (see Rom 8:26).

So according to no less an authority than Jesus, Christian prayer is to be to the Father, in the name of the Son, through the Spirit. And there is a logic to his instructions. Jesus is our great High Priest, the one who goes before us and makes our prayers to God the Father possible (see Heb 4:14–16). The Spirit is the one who leads, enables, and empowers our prayers. Christian prayer is a trinitarian exercise that would not work at all if God were more like Ant-Man than the triune God revealed in the Bible.

But isn't it OK to pray to Jesus? Don't we have examples of people in the Bible praying to Jesus? Not as many as you might think. I suppose that since Jesus is the Son of God, every time anyone spoke to Jesus, he or she was, in a sense, praying. But I am not sure that really counts; otherwise when the disciples asked Jesus to pray, he would have told them they were already praying when they asked the question.[4] Stephen, the first Christian martyr, called out to Jesus as he was dying (Acts 7:56–59), and Paul spoke to Jesus on the road to Damascus (Acts 9:5), but both Stephen and Paul actually saw Jesus as they spoke to him. Paul did pray to Jesus, asking him to heal him of the "thorn in the flesh" (2 Cor 12:7–8). And that pretty much exhausts the biblical examples of people praying to Jesus.

So, is it OK to pray to Jesus or even to the Spirit? Praying to Jesus and praying to the Spirit is praying to God, and I am sure that the members of the Trinity can sort it out. But as for me, I prefer to follow Jesus's instructions. Pray to the Father, in the name of Jesus, in and through the Spirit.

Ant-Man Cannot Save You. I mentioned in chapter 1 that sin is a human problem that requires a human solution. I also mentioned in chapter 2 that only God can save us. Those two facts create a problem. If humans have sinned against God, then God is rightly angry at us. Given that God is also the very standard of justice, the one who must and will judge all his moral agents whom he created, we are in a terrible fix. God cannot look the other way. He is too holy.

Also, contrary to the opinions of many, God cannot just forgive. That would be to deny himself as the holy God. He has to judge sin. He has to uphold the moral fabric of the universe.

There is another serious problem with "just forgiving." It would make us out to be people who just don't matter, people not to be taken seriously. Think about it. If God said to our rebellion against him, "No problem. No big deal," he would effectively be telling us that we are no more significant than

---

[4] Jesus would have said that too, if he'd thought it were true. Remember his response when Philip asked him to show them the Father. "Um, guys, if you have seen me, you have seen the Father. I've been with you this long and you ask a question like that? Come on!" (John 14:9, my translation).

insects, that what we do doesn't really matter. But God does take us seriously. Our moral decisions really do count. God has given to us the incredible privilege of actually mattering. But it comes with a price, a price that we are absolutely unable to pay.

Thankfully, God took matters into his own hands. God the Father, the Judge of the cosmos, sent the Son to be like us and to die in our place. To actually live as one of us (and not like Superman, someone who only seemed to be like us), the Son had to live in dependence upon the Holy Spirit (more on this in chapter 5). Further, Jesus lived a life of submission to his Father; he did not submit to himself ("For I have come down from heaven, not to do my own will but the will of him who sent me," John 6:38). In order to do that as a legitimate human, he trusted and depended on the Holy Spirit; he did not depend upon himself ("God anointed Jesus of Nazareth with the Holy Spirit," Acts 10:38).

While hanging on the cross, Jesus cried out, "My God, my God, why have you abandoned me?" (Matt 27:46)—a strange thing to lament if you are just talking to yourself. Just before he died, Jesus prayed, "Father, into your hands I entrust my spirit" (Luke 23:46). Again, if God is like Hank Pym, then this is like Ant-Man trying to talk to Giant-Man, which makes no sense. But if Jesus is an entirely different person from the Father, then it is right and good that the Son would offer himself up to the Father, because that is how the gospel works.

The apostle Paul drilled into the logic of the gospel in Rom 3:23–26:

> For all have sinned and fall short of the glory of God, and are justified by his grace as a gift, through the redemption that is in Christ Jesus, whom God put forward as a propitiation by his blood, to be received by faith. This was to show God's righteousness, because in

his divine forbearance he had passed over former sins.
It was to show his righteousness at the present time, so
that he might be just and the justifier of the one who has
faith in Jesus. (ESV)

Look closely at Paul's words. The word "justified" means to
be declared righteous, innocent, or not guilty. Sinners like you
and me are declared, in God's court of justice, to be not guilty,
to be righteous. God is able to do this, not by taking a legal
shortcut or "just forgiving." No, God is able to forgive and still
be holy God because the Father sent Christ Jesus, the incarnate
Son of God, to pay the penalty for human sin. The word "propitiation" is an important word, and it basically means to turn
away wrath or anger. Jesus propitiated God the Father. Jesus,
the Son of God, turned away God's righteous wrath against sin.
He completely satisfied all the moral indignation and judgment
against sin that our rebellious actions brought about in the heart
of our holy God.

The rest of the Romans passage is vitally important. Notice
it says that Jesus had to come "because in his [God's] forbearance he had passed over former sins." Let me tell you what this
means.

Suppose that an alien tribunal had come, during Old
Testament times, to judge the way God was governing the universe (such a thing is actually impossible, but work with me).
This tribunal saw that God's special creations, his image bearers, men and women, had rebelled against him. They would
have known that such creatures deserved to be judged and condemned. (God himself had declared the penalty for sin—death.)
And yet, they continued to live, some of them under God's
blessing. Sure, the tribunal would have seen that sacrifices were
being offered for sin; lots of animals were dying in the place
of people. But the tribunal would also have known that a bull,

lamb, or goat cannot pay the penalty for human sin. The penalty for human sin is human death. So this make-believe alien tribunal would have said to God, "You are not perfect. You are not holy. You can't just forgive. You are passing over all these sins as though they do not matter! You can't do that because they do matter!"

God could and would have responded, "You are right. Those sins do matter. But I am not compromising, nor am I 'just forgiving.' I can forgive because my Son will pay the penalty for sin completely in my perfect timing" (see Gal 4:4; 1 Tim 2:6; Mark 1:15).

It might have seemed that God was "passing over former sins" back in the Old Testament times. Lots of sheep were dying, but those really don't count. Look at Heb 10:4: "For it is impossible for the blood of bulls and goats to take away sins." But God was able to forgive repentant sinners, even before Christ came, because the Father knew that Jesus would come and die for sin.

Why does God need to be triune to do this? Why can't God be like Hank Pym and just play a different role or put on a different costume depending on the need? Because the need that the gospel meets required that all three persons of the Trinity play simultaneous roles. The Father is the God who sent the Son and condemned sin at the cross. The Son is the God who became a man, inaugurated a kingdom, and offered himself up for sin. The Spirit is the God who enabled and empowered the incarnate Son to live an authentically human life and then raised the Son from the dead on the third day. And then the Spirit is the one who applies the work of Christ according to the will of the Father *to us*. All three play different and simultaneous roles that make the gospel what it is. The best news ever.

Ant-Man cannot save you; neither can Ant-Man Jesus. But the Jesus revealed in the Bible can, and he can do much more.

DISCUSSION QUESTIONS

QUESTIONS FOR PERSONAL REFLECTION

- When you think of God, do you think of the one God, or the Father, Son, and Holy Spirit? Why?
- Does thinking about the Trinity give you a headache? Why should we work at understanding the Trinity?
- The Trinity is not an easy Christian doctrine, but it is important that we keep seeking the truth. Do you have a place where you can comfortably ask your questions about God?

QUESTIONS FOR GROUP DISCUSSION

- Is this group a good place to go with your questions about God?
- What illustrations of the Trinity have you heard? Where do they break down? How are they helpful? How might they be unhelpful?
- Which of the biblical arguments for the Trinity are most convincing and helpful to you? Why?
- How important is correctly understanding the Trinity to the Christian life?
- Why is it essential to the gospel that the Father, Son, and Holy Spirit be coexistent persons?
- Why is it essential to prayer that the Father, Son, and Holy Spirit be coexistent persons?
- To whom do you pray? Why? What will you change in your prayer life in light of what the author said in this chapter?

- What other biblical teachings are dependent upon the Father, Son, and Holy Spirit being three different and coexistent persons?

FOR FURTHER STUDY

Read Eph 1:3–14, a rich theological passage that speaks to the great blessing found in Jesus Christ. Consider the different roles played by the three members of the Trinity. Read through the passage again, noting all the pronouns. Try to determine in each case whether the pronoun refers to the Father, Son, or Holy Spirit.

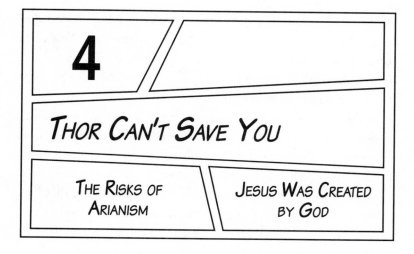

4

THOR CAN'T SAVE YOU

THE RISKS OF ARIANISM

JESUS WAS CREATED BY GOD

I am Thor Odinson of the Vikings, giant. I am not the god of reason and understanding. I am the god of Thunder and Lightning!!!
> —Thor in *Hulk* 2, no. 26 (December 2010)

In the beginning was the Word, and the Word was with God, and the Word was God.
> —John 1:1

My father was a master craftsman.

It seemed to me that he could make anything he wanted with whatever material or tool was handy. His best medium, though, was wood, and in his hands a hammer was a precision instrument.

In my hands, a hammer was something more like a weapon of mass destruction.

Together, my father and I worked on quite a few projects. We built home additions, installed roofs, made furniture, and remodeled rooms. We were quite a team, my dad and I. I took care of the tasks consistent with my skills: I held wood and handed my dad tools. My father did everything else. This division of labor worked well, though at times I tried to help in more substantial ways and usually just jeopardized the project.

I remember watching with awe as my dad drove nails straight and true. When it was my turn, I usually bent more nails than I drove. One time, when we were putting a roof on our new family room, he actually started all the nails for me, leaving nice lines of nails waiting for me to just tap them in the rest of the way. Even I was capable of completing that task with minimal damage. Before long, I got cocky. Not only was I pounding all the nails in, but I was able to drive them all the way in with only one or two blows. I had never enjoyed that kind of success with a hammer before. It was not long before I was adrift in the world of fantasy, pretending that I was the comic book hero Thor, wielding my mighty hammer, Mjolnir, with speed, power, and accuracy. The nails became evil aliens, and the roof was the world I was trying to save.

I was only the destruction of a few bad guys away from saving the universe when my father came back and asked me what I was doing. A bit disturbed that I had to explain the obvious, I told him I was ridding the earth of invaders. He replied that it looked more like I was trying to ruin the roof. I had left a swath of destruction, all right, but only in terms of bent nails and ruined shingles. A small price to pay, in my book, for eliminating so many evil aliens, but not exactly what my father was looking for in roof construction.

I went back to handing my dad shingles and nails.[1]

---

[1] To add insult to injury, my father took all my bent nails and hammered them straight into the shingles, leaving behind no evidence that I had even been there, much less that I had just saved the cosmos. Even so, I really miss my dad.

And then I went to my Thor comics to study up on proper hammer technique.

According to Marvel, the hero Thor is the son of Odin, the god and ruler of Asgard. Odin and his brothers were the creators of Earth (they called it Midgard), and above it they created a world for themselves called Asgard. Eventually, Thor is born to Odin and Gaia, a primal earth goddess. Thor, being the son of Odin, is himself a god, an Asgardian, possessed of incredible strength. Armed with Mjolnir, his mighty hammer, he is able to fly and change the weather (think storms and lots of lightning).

Frustrated with Thor's proud attitude, Odin does what any good father would do—teach his son humility. He does this by sending Thor to earth and putting him in the body of a disabled medical student named Donald Blake, without memory or knowledge that he is actually an Asgardian god. (OK, not exactly what any good father would do.) Eventually, Thor recovers Mjolnir, discovers his true identity—at which point he is transformed back into the thunder god—and falls in love with an earth woman named Jane Foster. (Odin did not count on that.)

Thor, though, is not the only son of Odin. After defeating the frost giants, Odin finds the infant son of the frost giant king hidden in the snow and, driven by mercy, takes the child, Loki, and adopts him as his own son. But his father favors the biological son, Thor, because Loki does not possess any of the attributes valued by the other Asgardians, such as strength and valor. Instead, Loki is clever, but in a conniving and evil kind of way. He is a thorn in both Thor's and Odin's sides.

Thor possesses enormous power and strength. He became one of the original Avengers and was responsible for saving the earth on numerous occasions. But for all Thor's greatness, he is neither omnipotent nor omniscient. He is incredible, but not preeminent. He is the son of the creator of earth, Odin, but because he was born, there was a time when Thor did not exist. He is a god, but he is not *the* God.

And some people think the same of Jesus. He is the Son of God, *a* god, but not *the* God. The historic name of this bad idea is *Arianism*, but I call it the Thor heresy, and it has been around for a long time.

THE HERESY

During the first centuries after the death and resurrection of Jesus, the churches in various towns were run by bishops—the bigger the city and the church, the more prominent the bishop. A significant early church was founded in the Egyptian city of Alexandria, and during the late 200s and early 300s, the bishop of the church there was a man named Alexander. By all accounts, Alexander was a gentle soul and a good bishop.

Alexander had a presbyter (elder, church leader) in his congregation whose name was Arius (256–336). Arius greatly desired to be the bishop of Alexandria, and for a while he patiently bided his time, convinced that he was next in line. When Alexander stepped down or died, Arius would step into the role. It was bound to happen.

It was bound to happen, that is, until Alexander took on a young protégé named Athanasius and made him his assistant. Suddenly, Arius had a rival, and this did not sit well with him. As time passed, it became more and more obvious to Arius that Alexander favored Athanasius and if anyone were to succeed him, it was probably going to be Athanasius, not him. For the record, Athanasius brought much to the table when it came to bishop qualifications. History would demonstrate that Athanasius was one of the most able and influential leaders in the history of the church. But Arius was blind to this, seeing only a rival.

Arius figured that if things continued as they were, the people would follow Alexander's lead and Athanasius would be the next bishop. Arius's only hope was to try to discredit Alexander. If Alexander fell, then Athanasius would follow, clearing the way for Arius to take his rightful spot as bishop of Alexandria.

The best way to ruin Alexander, in Arius's estimation, was to paint him as a modalist, an advocate of what we called the Ant-Man heresy in the previous chapter. To clearly separate his position from that of Alexander, Arius proposed a theory of God that firmly separated Jesus from the Father. He began to teach that the Father and Son were so different that they were not only different persons, but were also different in essence. To make this even clearer, Arius proposed that the Father brought the Son into existence by creating him. By Arius's way of thinking, the difference between the Father and the Son was the difference between Creator and creature.

Arius did not deny that the Son was a god. The Son was certainly a god; he was just not *the* God. The Son was the first created being. After creating the Son, the Father used the Son to create everything else. The Father also sent the Son to be born as a human at Bethlehem. So the Father is eternal, but the Son is not. The Son is similar to the Father in essence, but he is not the same. Make no mistake about it: According to Arius, the Father was superior to the Son; the Son was inferior to the Father. God is God, and the Son is a god, greater than any human, but not quite so great as God the Father. Kind of like Thor: a god, but not *the* God.

Now, Alexander was no modalist, but he definitely was not going to go along with Arius's wild ideas either. So he attempted to rally other bishops to his cause and take a stand against the teaching (and politics) of Arius. At one point, he invited a bunch of bishops to Alexandria to decide the issue and make a clear unified statement against Arius.

Arius, however, was able to intimidate the bishops by inciting a riot. Crowds of people swarmed the city, carrying placards, singing, and chanting, "There was a time when the Son was not." (Thus hooliganism was born even before the advent of soccer.) The net effect was that Alexander was not able to rally the church at large to his side to make a clear statement against Arius's teaching.

Arius had a few things going for him. First, he was a very capable, persuasive, and attractive communicator. Arius could work a room and call people to his side.

Second, he had a few Bible verses that, taken in isolation, appeared to support his case. Passages such as Col 1:15, which says that Jesus Christ is the "firstborn over all creation," and any passage that calls Jesus the "only begotten Son" (John 3:16 KJV; see also John 1:14; Heb 1:5) seemed to teach that the Son came into being like most everybody else.

Third, and perhaps most important, his proposal was simple. As we discussed in chapter 3, the Trinity is difficult to explain. Arius's proposal was easy to understand: The Father created the Son. There was a time when the Son did not exist. The Son is inferior to the Father. Easy to understand, but neither accurate nor biblically faithful.

Arius's influence throughout the church was so great, and his ideas spread with such ferocity, that the church became unsettled. By this time, Christianity was well on its way to becoming the state religion of the Roman Empire. So, Constantine, the Roman emperor largely responsible for the Christianization of Rome, acted to bring some peace to the church. He could not have a controversy of this magnitude splitting his state religion.

At his own expense, Constantine convened a council of bishops, in 325, in the city of Nicaea (located in modern-day Turkey), to settle the Arian controversy. About 300 bishops made the trip, and it was a momentous event, because some of the church leaders bore the physical scars of the persecution that Constantine had only recently ended.

The bishops were divided into three groups. There were those loyal to Arius, who felt that the Father had a different essence than the Son; there was also a smaller group of bishops who saw Arianism as a threat to the Christian faith and wanted to clearly state that the Son has the same essence (*homoousios*) or nature as the Father; and then there was a large group of middle-ground bishops who wanted to bring an end to the dispute through compromise on both sides. Perhaps, these middle-ground bishops suggested, both sides could agree on the term "similar essence" (*homoiousios*). But to the anti-Arians, to be similar is not to be the same; to be similar is to be different, and they could not compromise.

Eventually, the bishops who felt that Arius was completely wrong won the day; Arius was exiled; and the council issued what is now known as the *Nicene Creed*.

We believe in one God, the Father Almighty, Maker of all things visible and invisible.

And in one Lord Jesus Christ, the Son of God, begotten of the Father the only-begotten; that is, of the essence of the Father, God of God, Light of Light, very God of very God, begotten, not made, being of one substance (*homoousios*) with the Father; by whom all things were made both in heaven and on earth; who for us men, and for our salvation, came down and was incarnate and was made man; he suffered, and the third

day he rose again, ascended into heaven; from thence he
shall come to judge the quick and the dead.

    And in the Holy Ghost.[2]

Notice the strong anti-Arian language. The Son was "begotten, not made." The Son is "of one being [*homoousios*] with the
Father." It was a clear and decisive victory by an outnumbered
group of bishops who were committed to holding steadfastly to
what the Bible teaches.

    One would think that when bishops gather from all over
the world at the request of the Roman emperor and they
issue a decisive and clear creedal statement, the Arian movement would fade away into obscurity. One would think
so, but unfortunately one would be wrong. In brief, here
is what happened: Athanasius did succeed Alexander as
bishop of Alexandria when he died just three years later in
328. Constantine, however, soon lifted Arius's exile, and the
majority of the church eventually became Arian, thanks in no
small part to the efforts of Constantine's heir, Constantius.
(Incredible! There was a time when most people in the church
thought that Jesus was more like Thor than like the remarkable
person testified to in the Scriptures.) Athanasius continued to
teach the Bible and the full deity of Jesus Christ, and for his
efforts was exiled multiple times. Toward the end of the fourth
century, the church again adopted the position championed
by Athanasius. Looking back, the great Christian theologian
Jerome commented during the 400s concerning the strange
Arian state of affairs one century earlier: "The entire world
woke from a deep slumber and discovered that it had become

---

[2] Philip Schaff, *The Creeds of Christendom, with a History and Critical notes,* History of the Creeds: Volume 1—Part 1 (New York: Cosimo, Inc., 2007), 28-29.

Arian."[3] Which only goes to show that when it comes to the theological positions of the church, the majority and politically powerful do not always win. The truth of God's Word will eventually prevail, and the kingdom of God will come on his terms, not on the terms of the world.

WHO COMMITS THE THOR HERESY TODAY?

The Thor heresy continues to be peddled today, thanks in large part to the efforts of Jehovah's Witnesses. There is not a lick of difference between what Jehovah's Witnesses believe about Jesus today and what Arius taught 1,700 years ago. You know this to be true if you have ever heard their knock on your door. Looking through the window and seeing a couple of people (usually at least one of whom is a woman—a key to knowing whether they are Mormon or JW) dressed in church attire, you have to make a choice. Do you want to engage them in discussion, or do you want to dismiss them by asking, "Didn't we take care of you guys back at Nicaea in 325?"[4] If you accept the challenge to engage, it will not be long before the differences in what you believe about Jesus rise to the surface.

The Jehovah's Witnesses/Thor heresy advocates will earnestly tell you that they believe that Jesus is the Son of God and that he is to be worshiped. But if you dig into the details, they will quickly tell you that the Son of God was created by the

---

[3] Justo L. Gonzalez, *The Story of Christianity, Volume 1: The Early Church to the Reformation*, revised and updated (HarperCollins: New York, 2010), 191.

[4] My wife's strategy is to ask them if she can pray for them. She is convinced speaking to the Lord about them is more effective than anything she could say to them. I suspect that she is correct. But I am a theology professor, so I feel obligated to engage them about who Jesus is. Kind of an occupational hazard, I suppose.

Father and that the Son is a god, but not *the* God—like Thor. He is, they believe, inferior to the Father. I can see the Jehovah's Witnesses' lips moving, but all I can hear is the hiss of Arius.

But you don't have to be a JW to fall prey to the Thor heresy. Christians can unwittingly fall into this deadly way of thinking anytime they think that the Son is inferior in essence to the Father, and that the Father is really the one who is God. How might this happen?

Have there been times in your life when your view of Jesus was not as high as what the Bible teaches? Maybe you know that Jesus is your great High Priest and that he sits at the right hand of the Father. But when confronted with the problems of the world, the suffering of others, or just the incredible difficulty in standing up for Jesus in our culture, you might ask yourself, *What can Jesus really do?*

There have been other times when I have considered the gargantuan task of world missions and what it will take to reach the enormous numbers of Muslims, Buddhists, and others across the globe. In my wrong thinking, I have wondered, *What will Jesus actually do for them? Is following Jesus worth the high price that conversion would demand they pay?* Without realizing it, I have reduced Jesus to little more than a small tribal deity, someone with some power in the Christian church, but not one who is worth giving up everything for. He might be *my* god, but is he really *the* God, the one before whom everyone must and should bow? Such thinking would be true of Thor, but it has nothing to do with Jesus.

WHAT THE BIBLE SAYS

The Scriptures present a view of Jesus that is much higher than anything described by the Thor heresy. One of Christ's closest followers, so close that in his Gospel record he referred to himself merely as "the disciple Jesus loved" (John 21:7, 20), described Jesus this way:

> In the beginning was the Word, and the Word was with God, and the Word was God. He was with God in the beginning. All things were created through him, and apart from him not one thing was created that has been created. In him was life, and that life was the light of men. (John 1:1–4)

The teaching here is profound, but it requires a bit of interpretation.

First off, who is "the Word"? John 1:14 says, "The Word became flesh and dwelt among us." The entire book of John is about Jesus, so we can safely assume that the one who "became flesh," that is, became human, was Jesus. Few would disagree with that (and by "few," I mean no one).

Second, before the Word became a man, when and where was he? Well, John starts off, "In the beginning . . ." I believe our minds are supposed to go to the other place in Scripture that begins, "In the beginning . . ."—Gen 1:1—the start of the entire thing. And we are told that at the start of the entire thing, the creation of the cosmos and the time-space continuum, the Word was with God.

I don't want to make your head hurt with Greek, but the form of the verb *to be* used in John 1—*was*—indicates action that had already been going. So "in the beginning," the Word already *was*, meaning he already existed. He was already there *before the beginning of it all*. Now, I am not sure what "before the beginning of time" even means, but we can be sure of this: John was teaching that at the point of creation, when everything started, the Word was already there.

Third, how can you be with God and also be God at the same time? Much of this book has been an answer to this very question, and the rest of the book will continue to provide an answer. Whoever the Word is, he is separate from God. That is, he can be with God. But the Word has been and continues simultaneously to be God. Recall our discussion of the Ant-Man heresy in the last chapter. Everything that it takes to be God, both God the Father and God the Son are. But the Son is not the Father. They are both God, but they are different persons. The Word is God and is with God.

Now, if a pair of Jehovah's Witnesses (modern-day Arian/Thor heresy advocates) comes and knocks on your door, and you choose to speak with them, it will not take long before the conversation turns to this passage. According to the New World Translation, the Jehovah's Witness Bible version, John 1:1 should be translated, "In the beginning was the Word, and the Word was with God, and the Word was a god."[5] Their translation makes the point that whoever the Word was, he might be a god, but he is not the God.

You need to know something: It is a terrible translation. In fact, no credible Greek scholars, be they Christian, agnostic, or atheist, think that this is a legitimate translation. It is dead wrong, and it was translated by JWs that way to prop up their Thor heresy theology.

I have tried to make that point when JWs come to my door. I tell them, "It is a lousy translation that no credible Greek scholar thinks is legitimate." They say, "No, it isn't lousy." I say, "Yes, it is." They say, "No, it's not." I say, "Yes, it is." They say, "No, it's not." I say, "Yes, it is." And then we repeat ourselves. After that, we repeat ourselves some more. It is frustrating.

---

[5] The New World Translation of John 1:1–4 reads: "In the beginning was the Word, and the Word was with God, and the Word was a god. This one was in the beginning with God. All things came into existence through him, and apart from him not even one thing came into existence. What has come into existence by means of him was life, and the life was the light of men" (Copyright 1961, 1970, 1981, 1984, 2013 Watch Tower Bible and Tract Society of Pennsylvania).

But let's read on. In chapter 2, I claimed that creating the cosmos was something that only God did, and if the Bible taught that the Son of God was responsible for creating, then that would mean that the Son was fully God. John 1:3 teaches precisely that.

Verse 3 states, "All things were created through him, and apart from him not one thing was created that has been created." How many things were made through the Word? The Greek word translated "all" means … "ALL." All things—literally everything that was made was made through the Word. If it was made, it was made through the Word. That means that there are two kinds of things in the world, two kinds of things that exist: things that are made and things that did the making. If you are made, then you are *not* one of the makers. More importantly, if you are one of the makers, you are *not* one of the things made. Think of it this way: If you took a sheet of paper, drew a line down the middle, and put things that are made on one side and things that did the making on the other side, you would have to put "The Word" on the side of things doing the making.

He can't be on both sides.

If all things were made through him, then he cannot be one of the things that was made. And if you are one of the things doing the making, then you are God. Not just a god, but *the* God.

It is as simple as that. And strangely enough, the New World Translation even translated 1:3 correctly. *Their own translation does not support what they purport to believe*, that the Son was created first, and then everything else was made through him.

Next, what about the claim that the Bible teaches that Jesus was the firstborn of the Father? Perhaps some of you memorized John 3:16 from the King James Version or the old NIV, which used the term "only begotten" to describe the Son. Doesn't "only begotten" mean that Jesus was born of the Father, and does that not imply that there was a time when the Son did not exist? And what about Col 1:15, which states that Jesus was the "firstborn over all creation"?

Let's go back to making our heads hurt with Greek. The Greek term that is sometimes translated "only begotten" is the word *monogenes*. Within Christian scholarly circles, there is some disagreement about the best way to translate this Greek term. Some believe that the best translation of *monogenes* is "unique" or "one and only." Look at Heb 11:17, where Isaac is referred to as the *monogenes* son of Abraham. We know that Isaac was neither the firstborn nor the only son of Abraham. Ishmael was the firstborn of Abraham, and there were many other children born after Isaac. But Isaac was the son of promise, which is what the verse affirms. In the same way, Jesus is the unique Son of promise of the Father. Others believe that "only begotten" is the best way to translate *monogenes* and that John 3:16 teaches, among many other things, the eternal sonship of Jesus Christ.[6]

But here is the crucial point: Whether you translate John 3:16 as "only begotten" or "unique" or "one and only," John has already demonstrated in the first two chapters of his Gospel that the Son of God is coeternal with God the Father. John could not have possibly meant that the Son was begotten in the sense that

---

[6] The Greek word *monogenes* is found in the Nicene Creed, which describes the Son as "only begotten" and specifies that the Son was begotten, not made. In saying this, the church taught that the Son is "eternally begotten" of the Father. That is, the Son eternally and continually derives his existence as the Son from the Father. The Father-Son relationship did not happen in a moment in time, but has always been, even before there was time. Admittedly, eternal begetting is a difficult and complex concept. But complex does not mean ridiculous. The church, unlike the Queen of Hearts in *Alice in Wonderland*, is not asking you to believe six impossible things before breakfast (or whenever you are reading this book). But what Christians must encourage one another to do is to believe within the parameters of what the Bible teaches. The Trinity is a glorious doctrine. How can it not be? But even in its glory it is still mysterious.

Arius taught, that the Son was the first created being, through whom everything else was created. The John who wrote 3:16 is the same John who wrote 1:1–4.

Colossians 1:15 states that Jesus is the "firstborn" over all creation. But does this term teach that Jesus was the first created being, as Jehovah's Witnesses and the rest of the Thor heresy advocates assert? In a word, no.

The very next verse (1:16) states that all things were created by the Son (more on this verse in a moment). Unless the Son was able to somehow create himself and then create everything else (a nifty trick, for sure), it cannot be that 1:15 teaches that the Son is the first created being. Rather, the Greek term *prototokos* indicates rank or supremacy. The word was used that way in Greco-Roman society and was also used in the Septuagint, the Greek translation of the Old Testament (see Ps 89:27, for example). The Son of God is not the greatest created being. He is far superior to that. He is the greatest being over all creation.

So, the so-called *only begotten* and *firstborn* passages do not teach that Jesus came into being, born by God the Father out of nonexistence. Such would be true of Thor when Odin fathered him, but not of the Son of God. He has always existed and is fully equal with the Father.

WHY IS THIS IMPORTANT?

So what is the harm in thinking that Jesus is like Thor—a god, but not the God? A Thor-like Jesus cannot save you, nor can he do all the things that the Bible says that Jesus has done, is doing, or will do.

You Were Created by, through, and for the Son. Paul made this exact point in Col 1:16 when he wrote, "For everything was created by him, in heaven and on earth, the visible and the invisible, whether thrones or dominions or rulers or authorities—all things have been created through him and for him." You cannot get clearer than that. All things were created by the Son. All things were created through and for the Son. And remember that word translated "all" means ALL (still a good translation).

If all things were created by, through, and for the Son, then *you* are included in the "all things." You and everyone else. That includes your family members who love Jesus and your family members who do not. It includes everyone who is part of your church and everyone who has never been a part of any church anywhere. It includes everyone in your hometown and everyone outside your city limits, to the very ends of the earth. *Everyone* was created by, through, and for the Son.

Jesus Christ is the Lord and King of all because he is the Creator of all and he has Creator's rights over everything he made.

Don't let anyone tell you that Jesus Christ is good enough for you but not great enough for most. Some people have said to me, "You only believe in Jesus because your parents do. But my family has different beliefs and we are doing fine." Such thinking permeates our postmodern world. After all, there are lots of options out there, a veritable smorgasbord, where you can sample religious entrees according to your tastes. In our postmodern world, religious commitment has been reduced to a matter of personal preference or what works best for individuals. And if Jesus were like Thor, a god but not the God, such thinking would be accurate and proper.

But you can have confidence that Jesus Christ has a claim on your unbelieving friends and family. Jesus is not some local tribal deity or family god. He is Lord and Creator of all. That does not mean that everyone will choose to follow Jesus, but it does mean that everyone should.

Because Jesus Christ is the God, and not simply a god, you can be sure that those who do not know Jesus would be better off serving him. You can be sure that Jesus Christ is just as relevant to the 12-year-old girl in Papua New Guinea as he is to your 70-year-old next-door neighbor in Portland. You can be sure that the deepest legitimate desires of all your unbelieving friends and family are truly met in Jesus Christ. No Thor-like Jesus can make that claim. But the Jesus Christ of the Bible can.

The Lord of the Universe Is Lord of the Church. So Jesus Christ is not just Lord of those who happen to follow him. He is the Lord of the cosmos, and he deserves and desires the allegiance of everybody.

But it is not as though the church is an afterthought or an annoying add-on to his already full list of God-responsibilities. For Jesus Christ, being Lord of the church is his passion; it is his priority, a vital aspect of his identity. Look again at Col 1:15–20.

> He is the image of the invisible God, the first-born over all creation. For everything was created by him, in heaven and on earth, the visible and the invisible, whether thrones or dominions or rulers or authorities—all things have been created through him and for him. He is before all things, and by him all things hold together. He is also the head of the body, the church; he is the beginning, the firstborn from the dead, so that he might come to have first place in everything. For God was pleased to have all his fullness dwell in him, and through him to reconcile everything to himself, whether things on earth or things in heaven, by making peace through his blood, shed on the cross. (vv. 17–20)

In this passage, Paul piled up the affirmations of the majesty and greatness of Jesus Christ. We have already looked at several of those affirmations: image of invisible God, firstborn of all creation, Creator of all things, the one in whom all things in the cosmos are reconciled to God, and so on. But I want you to notice that in the midst of these grand statements, we find this: "He is also the head of the body, the church" (1:18).

Paul made the exact same point in the same way in Eph 1:20–23, extolling the wonder of Jesus Christ before stating, "And he subjected everything under his feet and appointed him as head over everything for the church, which is his body."

Yes, Jesus is God incarnate. Yes, Jesus is the Savior of the world. And yes, Jesus is the head of the church, which Paul identified as the very body of Christ.

As Paul penned these words, I am sure his mind went back to the day he first met Jesus, the account of which is recorded in Acts 9:1–19.

Paul did not meet Jesus on a particularly good day. I suppose that any day that one sees Jesus and is saved is a good day, but if you were able to plan the perfect day to meet Jesus for the first time, you would probably want to be doing something godly, or at least not immoral. You definitely would not want to meet Jesus as you were on your way to persecute his followers. But that is precisely what Paul was doing. Armed with official letters from the Jewish leadership in Jerusalem, Saul (Paul's Hebrew name) was on his way to Damascus to arrest Jewish Christians when he first encountered Jesus.

To make matters worse, Paul discovered that by Jesus's way of thinking, to attack one of his followers is to attack him. Jesus takes such abuse very personally. His first words to Saul make this clear: "Saul, Saul, why are you persecuting me?" (Acts 9:4). Saul rightly asked the name of this authoritative figure and had to be terrified at the response: "I am Jesus, the one you are persecuting" (v. 5). Gulp!

What was horrifying at the time, Paul came to understand to be a fantastic truth. The Lord of the universe identifies himself with his people. And that is wonderful news.

The very one who is King of the cosmos is simultaneously the ruler and nurturer of the church. All the resources of God Almighty are at Jesus's disposal to lead and grow the church.

In the comics, Thor was often chided by the Asgardians for his strange devotion to the human Jane Foster. In their minds, Thor was neglecting his greater duties as a god of Asgard by wasting his time on Earth in his dalliance with the earth woman.

But Jesus's commitment to the church is no illegitimate preoccupation. The King of history, the one who holds the keys of life and death, understands himself to be Shepherd of his people, a people he loves. In fact, he refers to the church as his bride. The church is that special to him, that much of a priority. He came to establish a kingdom, to create a people for that kingdom, and then to nurture, guide, and grow them along the way. That is his mission.

And he is simultaneously the sovereign Lord.

At times it seems as though things are spinning out of control, going from bad to worse. As international terrorism escalates, natural disasters devastate, racial tensions rise, economic injustices grow, and so-called political solutions appear to be more and more counterproductive, it can be tempting for Christians to wonder if the Lord truly has his hand on the wheel.

But the biblical testimony is sure: The very one of whom it is said, "He is before all things, and by him all things hold together" (Col 1:17) is the same one who said, "I will build my church" (Matt 16:18). He is managing the cosmos, and he does so as head of the church. That means that in the good times and the bad, Jesus is building his church. Even when things look darkest, Jesus is on mission. When tsunamis and earthquakes strike, Jesus Christ is still saving and caring for a people. When the countries in North America and Europe struggle with Islamic terrorists, Jesus Christ is not taken by surprise, nor is he nervous. Is there evil in the world that violates Jesus's clear commands? Yes. Are there events and people that Jesus will judge when he returns to establish his kingdom? Absolutely. But even in the midst of the worst, Jesus is in control and is keeping his word. The headlines in New York and London, Tokyo and Sao Paulo may bemoan world calamities and conflicts, but the headlines in heaven consistently proclaim, "Jesus Is Lord, and He Is Building His Church!"

All That Jesus Is, He Is for You. The church that Jesus leads is no cold and faceless institution. It is made up of individuals, each one uniquely gifted by the Spirit of the Son of God to play a particular role of edification in the church, the body of Christ. Jesus knows each one of those members by name and died to reconcile each one to the Father. If you are a follower of the Lord Jesus Christ, know that the one who is Lord of the cosmos and Lord of the church is your Lord, personally and vitally.

The great theologian Garth Brooks is fond of crooning, "I've got friends in low places." Christian, you have a friend in the highest place imaginable. I suppose the Thor-like Jesus of the Arians is powerful, but he does not compare to the actual living Jesus, to whom the Bible testifies. If you have a friend in Jesus, you have a friend who is not just a god. He is *the* God, to whom belongs all strength, blessing, honor, and glory.

Thor cannot save you, but Jesus can.

DISCUSSION QUESTIONS

QUESTIONS FOR PERSONAL REFLECTION

- What difference does it make that Jesus Christ, the Savior, is also the one by, through, and for whom all things were made?
- Have you ever thought that Jesus was inferior in essence to the Father? Was that frightening or comforting? Why?
- Is Jesus majestic in your eyes because of what he has done for you, or is there a majesty to being the Son of God that exceeds anything that he has done? In other words, if the Son had not become a man and died for you, would you still recognize him as glorious?

QUESTIONS FOR GROUP DISCUSSION

- Have you ever had a Jehovah's Witness come to your door? Did you talk to him or her about Jesus? How did that go?
- Why is it important that the Son of God be equal to the Father?
- What kind of glory did Jesus have before the incarnation, before creation (John 17:5)?
- What difference does it make that the one who is your Savior is also the Creator?
- How important is the church if Jesus Christ, the Lord of all, sees himself as "head of the church" (Eph 5:23)? What impact should that have on the priority of the church in your life?

FOR FURTHER STUDY

Read Heb 1:1–4. What is the significance that the Son is (1) the one through whom God has spoken, (2) the one appointed as heir of all things, and (3) the one through whom the universe was created?

5

GREEN LANTERN CAN'T SAVE YOU

| THE AGONIES OF ADOPTIONISM | JESUS WAS A GOOD MAN ADOPTED BY GOD |

With that ring I'm probably the most powerful man on earth.

> —Hal Jordan in *Emerald Dawn* 1, no. 2
> (January 1990)

God anointed Jesus of Nazareth with the Holy Spirit and with power, and . . . he went about doing good and healing all who were under the tyranny of the devil, because God was with him.

> —The apostle Peter (Acts 10:38)

Much of life is devoted to pursuing rings. Not necessarily because of what they actually are, but because of what they represent. Rings are symbols of the fulfillment of our greatest dreams and commitments. Whether they be class rings, championship rings, wedding rings, or just gaudy, sparkly rings that show off wealth and misplaced priorities, there are very few people who have not been motivated by the prospect of receiving and wearing a ring of some kind. Rings have always been powerful symbols, and this is largely regardless of culture or time.

So it is only natural that rings would become powerful talismans in stories and legends. Of course, the greatest use of rings was by J. R. R. Tolkien in his epic trilogy and my all-time favorite book, *The Lord of the Rings*.[1] In it, rings of power figure prominently, and the entire story is dedicated to the destruction of "the One Ring," a device of power so great and evil that the only hope for Middle Earth is to destroy it.

For my own part, I have desired only three kinds of rings: I happily wear a wedding ring that symbolizes my marriage and commitment to my wife; it has been at least a couple of years since I outgrew my need for a secret decoder ring; and I am still waiting on a ring that grants me superpowers.

Superheroes are no strangers to rings of power. They provide an opportunity for otherwise ordinary human beings to be granted incredible power and abilities. The most famous example of such a superhero is DC's Green Lantern.

Hal Jordan, Green Lantern's alter ego, was a good guy by anyone's standards: brave, honest, and compassionate. As a

---

[1] Warning: I am one of those nerds who has read *The Lord of the Rings* at least a dozen times. I first read it as a sixth grader when I was loaned the trilogy (thanks, Uncle Dex—you changed my life!), received my own copy for Christmas my seventh-grade year (thanks, Mom and Dad!), read it annually through college, and have read the trilogy out loud in its entirety twice since (thanks for listening, Natalie, Ethan, and Levi, and then Julius, Vicente, and Marcos!). I am so familiar with the story that it is the only book that I pick up and read at various places for the mere enjoyment of reading specific chapters. The volumes are faithful friends that sit on my shelf and are always kind to me. My favorite chapter in the trilogy is "The Houses of Healing" in *The Return of the King*. When the future king Aragorn enters the capital city of Gondor incognito and is recognized by a few because "the hands of the king are the hands of a healer, and so shall the rightful king be known," it makes me yearn for the return of Jesus.

child, he idolized his father, Martin Jordan, a test pilot for Ferris Aircraft. But when young Hal witnessed his father's death in a plane crash, he was traumatized. His lifelong plan to follow in his father's footsteps was severely tested. In an act of extraordinary courage, Hal swallowed his fear and enlisted in the U.S. Air Force immediately after his eighteenth birthday, eventually becoming a test pilot himself for his father's old company.

Meanwhile, the universe is continuously protected by an intergalactic police force known as the Green Lantern Corps. Each member of this select group of beings from different planets across the cosmos is empowered by a ring, an amulet of incomprehensible power that is controlled by the will of the bearer. The one wearing the ring can do pretty much anything, creating whatever the bearer wishes out of pure "Oan" energy — energy from the planet Oa, where the rings originated. The only limitations are the imagination, skill, and, most important, will of those who wield the rings.[2]

So it follows that Oan energy is really just a tangible form of willpower. The ring does have to be "recharged" periodically by a green lantern (hence the name of the Superhero), which links the ring to the original power source on Oa. The recharging is not instantaneous, so the Green Lanterns typically pass the time by reciting the Green Lantern oath.[3] The oath is not a magical formula, but is really a sort of creed that serves to steel the ring bearer's will for future missions.

---

[2] The power of the ring is strangely susceptible to the color yellow also, but since yellow is not the color of choice for most bad guys, the ring bearer is good to go. One prominent exception is Sinestro, a rogue Green Lantern, who wields a power ring that uses yellow energy (yellow being the color of fear).

[3] "In brightest day, in blackest night, no evil shall escape my sight. Let those who worship evil's might, beware my power, Green Lantern's light" (*Green Lantern* no. 9, fall 1943). OK, it's a little bit on the dramatic side, but it's more superheroish than whistling.

Unbeknownst to Jordan, one member of the Green Lantern Corps, named Abin Sur, was mortally wounded while on mission, forcing an emergency landing on the nearest planet, Earth. The dying Sur knew that he had to find a replacement, so he used the ring to find an earthling who had the courage and character necessary to be a member of the Corps. Out of all the people on Earth, the ring found Jordan, who took the ring, joined the Green Lantern Corps, and eventually became a founding member of the Justice League of America, DC Comics' superhero team.

There are two very important points to remember about Green Lantern: First, the secret to Green Lantern's power is the ring. Jordan has courage and strength and other human attributes we commonly associate with heroism, but what makes him a superhero is the ring. Apart from it, Hal Jordan is just a man.

But with the ring, what a hero he is. The Green Lantern rings are commonly understood to be the most powerful weapons in the entire DC universe. They appear to be omnipotent since a limit to what they can do has never been found. They are able to construct anything that the bearer imagines from that distinctive strange green energy. Green Lantern uses the ring to fly and to do all of his fighting. The ring can channel energy and bend light waves, rendering the superhero invisible. By his merely thinking of something, the ring creates it, whether it be a giant fist or an energy gun with seemingly unlimited range. The objects created only last as long as the superhero wills them to do so.

Second, it is important to remember that the ring found and chose Hal Jordan due to his character, courage, and the strength of his will. Not just anybody can be a superhero. It takes a unique person, with very specific qualities, and not every planet can boast of qualified applicants. When Jordan was selected, it was determined that there were only one or two others on the entire planet eligible to bear the ring. In the case of Jordan, the act of swallowing his fear and hopping into the cockpit of a plane, despite his family tragedy, set him apart from everybody else. He had demonstrated a will of steel and was thus worthy to wear the talisman.

So Hal Jordan, a human being, was given a source of remarkable and seemingly limitless power due to his character, courage, and strength of will. And by this time you will not be surprised to hear that many people have the same idea about Jesus. To them, Jesus was a regular human being possessed of extraordinary piety and devotion to God. Because of that piety, God chose Jesus, adopted him as his son, and gave him a "talisman of power," the Holy Spirit. Armed and directed by the Spirit of God, Jesus did amazing things for God throughout his life, until his mission was ended by his death on the cross.

I call such thinking the Green Lantern heresy, and it has been around for a very long time. In fact, it is probably the earliest of the bad ideas about Jesus.

THE HERESY

There have been many versions of the Green Lantern heresy throughout history, but they all fall under the name "Adoptionism."[4] Another name is "dynamic monarchianism" which translated means "power of the one Ruler." Whatever we call it, all the versions share two things in common.

---

[4] The proper spelling is Adoptianism, but most today spell the word, Adoptionism because of the word *adoption*. Theologians often struggle to avoid being esoteric.

First, Jesus was the *son of God*, not because of any divine essence within Jesus, not because of the incarnation, but because God adopted him to be such. Before the adoption, Jesus was a pious but otherwise ordinary man. After his adoption as the son of God, he was still an ordinary man. So how did Jesus do all the extraordinary things that he did? The answer lies in the Spirit of God.

Second, upon his adoption, Jesus was given the *power of God*, something that gave him special and unique abilities. There was nothing in Jesus himself that enabled him to do anything amazing, much less miraculous. Like Hal Jordan, who was empowered by the ring, Jesus received his supernatural ability thanks only to a special manifestation of the power of God. What was Jesus's talisman of power? The Spirit of God.

Here is how Adoptionism began: Almost immediately after Paul, John, and the rest of the apostles died, the church started to wrestle with the issue of how Jesus Christ related to God. A group of second-century Jewish Christians, known as the Ebionites, taught that Jesus Christ was just a man who was adopted by God. God's adoption of Christ was a designation coupled with some divine empowerment. Remember that the Jewish people are historically strident monotheists, so accepting Jesus as fully divine, the Son of God, was and is difficult for them. To their understanding, if Jesus is God, then there must be two Gods, and that was unacceptable.

The Ebionites argued that the moment of Jesus's adoption was his baptism, an event recorded in all four Gospels, when God declared from heaven, "This is my beloved Son" (Matt 3:17), and then sent the Spirit to empower Jesus for his ministry. As is the case with most of the Adoptionists, the Ebionites did not believe that the Spirit was a personal being, but was instead just a manifestation of the power of God (much like Green Lantern's ring). The Ebionites also believed that followers of

Jesus should obey the Mosaic law. However, once the letters of the apostles began to circulate, letters like Paul's epistle to the Galatians, Ebionism was doomed.[5]

Adoptionism did not die with the Ebionites. It was taught by a guy named Theodotus in the late 100s and another named Artemon in the early 200s. A more prominent form of Adoptionism was then proposed by Paul of Samosata, the bishop of Antioch later in the third century. Paul of Samosata allegedly taught that Jesus was born of the virgin Mary by the Holy Spirit and was later united with the second member of the Trinity, someone Paul of Samosata called "the *Logos*." So we have a morally excellent but merely human Jesus united with God and empowered for ministry.

Paul of Samosata was excommunicated in 268 for his views, but, for the record, he had other issues as well. He had a throne erected in the church building for himself, always maintained an entourage of bodyguards, and changed the lyrics of the church's praise songs, substituting his own name for that of Jesus. So the need for bodyguards probably makes some sense. (Church history is so full of crazies that it should never be boring. If you are bored with church history, blame your teachers, not the material!)

Modern-day Adoptionists (or Green Lantern heretics) are the Unitarians. Unitarian beliefs can be traced back to the late 1500s, when an Italian man named Lelio Sozzini, and his nephew Fausto Sozzini, dismissed the Trinity, teaching that there is only one God—God the Father. To them, talk of an incarnation and Jesus being fully man and fully divine was impossible to reconcile with modern science and philosophy (or whatever the

---

[5] Pretty much the entirety of the book of Galatians is dedicated to persuading Gentile Christians that they do not have to follow Jewish law to be a part of the family of God.

1500s versions of science and philosophy were). They denied the preexistence of the Son of God. To them, Jesus was a mere man who was adopted by God and then endowed with divine powers. The Sozzinis did teach that Jesus eventually died on the cross, but not to atone for human sin. Instead, his death was exemplary, merely an example of what living for God is worth. Christ's death did bring about forgiveness on the part of God, but not because Jesus's death paid an actual penalty for sin. (How could it, if Jesus Christ is not God?) Rather, Christ's death was put forward by God to show what he thought of sin, and trust in Christ became the condition of God's forgiveness. Why? No other reason was given other than because God said so.

The Sozzinis did not fare much better than other false teachers, though they created a big enough stink that they did have a heresy named after them—Socinianism. The Socinians did not have the benefit of a burly entourage, as Paul of Samosata did. Instead, they had to flee. They found refuge in Transylvania (of Dracula fame—no, I am not making this up) and later in Raków, Poland. Their followers grew into a sect, and their teaching was eventually written up in the *Racovian Catechism*. (If the Socinians had written the catechism from Transylvania instead of Raków, we would have the *Transylvanian Catechism*. And that would be a title creepy enough to match the danger of their ideas.)

WHO COMMITS THE GREEN LANTERN HERESY TODAY?

The Socinian beliefs spread across western Europe and eventually made their way across the Atlantic to North America, taking the moniker *Unitarian*. The Unitarian name indicates the denial of the Trinity and the commitment to the oneness or "unity" of God. The Unitarian church in America got started in the 1700s and included such luminaries as presidents John Adams and his son, John Quincy Adams, as well as Ralph Waldo Emerson and Harriet Beecher Stowe. The Unitarian church still exists today. They prefer to call themselves "Unitarian" rather than "Socinian," because putting the name of an old heresy on your church building is bad for business, a violation of seeker-sensitive strategies. Though they call themselves Unitarian, I prefer to call them Green Lantern heretics. (Though I could probably be talked into calling them "Transylvanians.")

Unitarianism shares a lot in common with the Batman heresy (Christian liberalism), which we discussed in chapter 2. There are variations of Unitarianism, but all share an over-emphasis on there being one God (monotheism) that leads to a denial that there are three persons in the Godhead (the Trinity). To Unitarians, Jesus Christ was a good man, an incredible teacher, and a wonderful life model who was uniquely empowered by God to do remarkable things (perhaps even some miracles, though most will say that they cannot be sure). Many modern Unitarians who have drifted from the teachings of the Socinians are also Universalists, believing that everybody will be saved regardless of religion, morality, life choices, or whether they have repented and believed in Christ.

But you do not have to be a member of a Unitarian church to fall prey to the Green Lantern heresy.

If you like Jesus and think he did miraculous things, but do not think that he was really God, you have landed in Green Lantern heresy territory.

If you acknowledge that Jesus Christ died for sins (but do not really know how), but wonder whether Jesus has what it takes to do much else with the evil in the world, you are probably dabbling in the Green Lantern heresy.

If you read the biblical passages that speak of Jesus being guided by the Holy Spirit or doing his miracles by the Holy

Spirit and conclude that these are proof that Jesus was not divine, then you are squarely within the realm of the Green Lantern heresy.

And here is why . . .

WHAT DOES THE BIBLE SAY?

The Scriptures paint a very different picture from that portrayed by the various advocates of the Green Lantern heresy. We have already covered in great detail the biblical teaching on the deity of the Son (see chapters 2–4). In those chapters, we learned that the Son of God is eternally the divine Son, coequal and coeternal with God the Father and God the Holy Spirit. (We say "coequal" to demonstrate that the Son is completely equal in essence and divinity to the Father and the Spirit. We say "coeternal" to demonstrate that there has never been a time when the Son was not coequal with the Father and the Spirit.)

But the biblical teaching on the deity of the Son is not limited to what we have covered to this point. Far from it. Another crucial teaching is that Jesus was (and is) fully divine and yet was still dependent upon the Spirit of God.

Jesus Was Fully Divine. Paul addressed the issues that would be raised by the Green Lantern heresy full on when he wrote a letter to the church in Philippi. Apparently, the church in that first-century Macedonian city was struggling with disunity and pride. To counter this, Paul instructed:

> Adopt the same attitude as that of Christ Jesus, who, existing in the form of God, did not consider equality with God as something to be exploited. Instead he emptied himself by assuming the form of a servant, taking on the likeness of humanity. And when he had come as a man, he humbled himself by becoming

obedient to the point of death—even to death on a cross. (Phil 2:5–8)

Let's break the passage down phrase by phrase:

Adopt the same attitude as that of Christ Jesus . . . Paul did not initially sit down to explain the ins and outs of the deity of Christ. But in response to a messy relational problem, Paul appealed to the person of Jesus. This is instructive because it tells us that theology matters. What we know about Jesus is not just important for winning a trivia game; what we know about Jesus affects the way we act. Paul's instructions are clear: Be like Jesus. In particular, be humble like Jesus. And to explain just how humble Jesus Christ actually was, Paul dove straight into the deep end of the theological pool.

Who, existing in the form of God . . . Before Jesus Christ was born as a fully human baby in Bethlehem, the Son of God existed as God. The word "form" is best understood as essence. As I explained earlier, everything that it took to be God, the Son possessed. He was (and is) completely and fully God.

. . . did not consider equality with God as something to be exploited. Instead, he emptied himself . . . The Son enjoyed equality with God; that is, he had all the trappings and privileges of deity, the existence of divinity, being himself fully God. Imagine all the glory, honor, and majesty that rightly belong to the one who is God. Recall from chapter 2 the throne room of heaven, with fantastic beings created to praise and worship God. All this belonged to the Son. It was part of his everyday experience. But Paul taught that the Son did not leverage the fact that he was God for his own benefit, to avoid a tough assignment. Instead, we are told that the Son "emptied" himself. In the Greek language, the word translated "emptied" usually meant "poured out," like what we would do with a pitcher of water.

Here is where it gets sticky. How did the Son of God "empty" himself? Does it mean that he stopped being divine? Does it mean that he divested himself of divine attributes? There have been some throughout history who have believed that this is exactly what Paul meant. During the 1800s, a group of men explicitly taught that the Son stopped being God when he became man, and they based it on this verse.[6] There are two problems with this interpretation. First, as we will soon see, it is not what Paul actually taught; and second, if the Son had stopped being God when he became a man, then we are basically right back at the Batman heresy (and we already debunked that bad idea about Jesus in chapter 2).

No, rather than thinking that the Son divested himself of divine attributes, thereby ceasing to be God, we should keep reading in Philippians, because Paul tells us exactly how the Son of God "emptied" himself.

. . . *by assuming the form of a servant, taking on the likeness of humanity. And when he had come as a man* . . . Paul used three phrases to describe how Jesus emptied himself. Notice that in each case he "emptied" himself by adding to himself.

First, he took on the form of a servant. The word *form* is repeated, and we should again think of essence. Jesus took on the very nature, essence, and existence of a servant. That is, he became a true servant in every sense of the word.

Second, Jesus took on, was born in, the likeness of humanity. Like every human being after Adam and Eve, Jesus was born. As we discussed in chapter 1, Jesus's virgin conception was extraordinary, but he was formed in the womb for nine

---

[6] The emptying of the Son of God referred to in Phil 2:7 is called the *kenosis*, after the Greek word used in the passage that is translated "empty." We call the bad idea about Jesus giving up his deity, in the kenosis, the kenotic heresy. I have not found a superhero who specifically embodies this bad idea. If you know of one, let me know!

months or so, like every other baby, and he was born (albeit with accompanying angelic choir) just like every other baby.

Third, Jesus came as a man. Literally, the text says, "being discovered in appearance as a man." Jesus's humanity was not a secret. It was there for all to see. The verdict on Jesus by all who saw and knew him was that he was what he appeared to be—a man.

Notice what Paul did *not* write: He did not write that Jesus emptied himself by giving up his divine nature and *replacing* it with a human nature. Rather, Jesus "emptied" himself by *adding* a human nature to himself. It was, if you will, subtraction by addition.

My professor and mentor Dr. Bruce Ware illustrates the concept of subtraction by addition in this way: Consider a brand-new Ferrari sitting in an auto showroom.[7] The car is in mint condition, and the paint shines with a luster that magnifies all the power and glory of an expensive sports car. Now imagine somebody taking it for a test drive on a rainy day. But he does not stay on paved roads. He decides to check what is under the hood by taking the vehicle off-road. Not taking the time to run the car through a car wash, the driver returns the car caked in mud. The shine, glory, and luster of the car are now hidden by a thick layer of dirt. The car is still as powerful as before. Nothing has been taken away. But the glory is diminished (or veiled) by the addition of earthly sediment. Subtraction by addition.

He humbled himself by becoming obedient to the point of death—even to death on a cross. Because Jesus took the very essence, nature, and existence of a servant, we should expect that Jesus would do the deeds consistent with a servant. In

---

[7] You can find this illustration and others in Bruce Ware's excellent book, *The Man Christ Jesus: Theological Reflections on the Humanity of Christ* (Wheaton, IL: Crossway, 2013), 20–23.

obedience to the decree of God the Father, the Son of God became a human and then kept on obeying the Father his entire life to the very end. And the end of his life was costly. Jesus obeyed the Father all the way to the cross.

Socinians, Unitarians, Adoptionists, and other advocates of the Green Lantern heresy would have you believe that Jesus was incredibly pious but just a mere human before his adoption as the Son. But Paul corrected that assertion by teaching that Jesus Christ existed as the Son both before and during the incarnation.

This is not to deny that the Holy Spirit was active in the life of Jesus Christ. Far from it, Jesus depended on the Holy Spirit to enable and empower his ministry. In fact, his very name and title, Jesus Christ, points to the priority of the Spirit in the life and ministry of Jesus.

Jesus Christ, Though Fully Divine, Depended on the Spirit of God. If you were to ask the people in your church, "What is it that makes Jesus the Christ?" what would they say? That he was the Son of God? He was the Son of David? He was the rightful King? All those answers are important facts, but none of them makes Jesus the Christ.

The names *Christ* and *Messiah* are based on transliterations of the Greek and Hebrew words, respectively, that mean "Anointed One." So Jesus is the Christ or Messiah because he was the Anointed One. But anointed with what?

In the Old Testament, when the Lord wanted to publicly designate someone for a missional office, he would have him anointed. Kings (most notably Saul in 1 Samuel 10 and David in 1 Samuel 16); priests (most notably Aaron and the priests in Exodus 30); and prophets (most notably Elisha in 1 Kings 19) were installed or consecrated through anointing with oil. In Israel's economy, to be publicly anointed for ministry was a huge deal because it gave your calling gravitas and durability.

Keep in mind that David refused to lift his hand against King Saul because he was "the LORD's anointed," literally, "the Lord's Messiah" (e.g., 1 Sam 24:6; 26:9; 2 Sam 1:14; etc.).

So, it should come as no surprise that the Old Testament prophets pinned their hopes on a future anointed one, a champion, a king, a messiah, who would initiate the day of the Lord and save Israel. But it is with what, or should we say with whom, the Coming One is anointed that is eye-opening. The future savior of Israel would be anointed, not with oil, but with the Spirit of God. And the result would be marvelous.

Isaiah, some 700 years before the birth of Jesus, prophesied:

> Then a shoot will grow from the stump of Jesse, and a branch from his roots will bear fruit. The Spirit of the LORD will rest on him—a Spirit of wisdom and understanding, a Spirit of counsel and strength, a Spirit of knowledge and of the fear of the LORD. His delight will be in the fear of the LORD. He will not judge by what he sees with his eyes, he will not execute justice by what he hears with his ears, but he will judge the poor righteously and execute justice for the oppressed of the land. He will strike the land with a scepter from his mouth, and he will kill the wicked with a command from his lips. Righteousness will be a belt around his hips; faithfulness will be a belt around his waist. (Isa 11:1–5)

Note the enormous role that the Spirit is supposed to play in this future son of Jesse, a new and better David. The Spirit would bring wisdom, understanding, counsel, strength, knowledge, and fear of the Lord. These are all attributes that would be necessary to do all that the Lord required. Isaiah says much the same thing in 42:1–9, but it is what he predicted in chapter 61 that is the most gripping.

The Spirit of the Lord GOD is on me, because the LORD
has anointed me to bring good news to the poor. He has
sent me to heal the brokenhearted, to proclaim liberty
to the captives and freedom to the prisoners; to proclaim the year of the LORD's favor, and the day of our
God's vengeance. (Isa 61:1–2)

When Jesus began his public ministry, he went to the synagogue in his hometown of Nazareth (see Luke 4:16–37). By this
time, there was a buzz about Jesus that was circulating throughout Galilee. People were talking about Jesus's teaching. So when
he showed up at the synagogue, it was only right that he be
asked to teach. Receiving the scroll of Isaiah, Jesus turned to
Isaiah 61 and began to read. Everybody who was in attendance
had probably heard this passage so many times they knew it by
heart. It contained promises that were the fulfillment of Israel's
greatest dreams. Think of it as the primary text of a Jewish Hope
101 class. One day the Lord would raise up one who, empowered by the Spirit, would bring peace, relief, and consolation
to Israel by bringing about the day of God's vengeance on his
enemies. The Jewish people had suffered at the hands of foreign
authoritarian rule for too long, but that would all end when the
Lord sent his champion.

Strangely, Jesus stopped quoting Isaiah 61 in the middle of
verse 2, finishing in the middle of a sentence, leaving out the
part about proclaiming "the day of our God's vengeance" and
an additional clause, "to comfort all who mourn." Then he
methodically "rolled up the scroll, gave it back to the attendant,
and sat down. And the eyes of everyone in the synagogue were
fixed on him" (Luke 4:20). You could have cut the tension and
anticipation in the air with a knife. What would he say? Jesus
did not disappoint.

"Today as you listen, this Scripture has been fulfilled" (4:21).

What Jesus said was nothing less than "Israel, your wild-est hopes and dreams have come true. Your prayers have been answered. The deepest desires of your hearts have been ful-filled. The Spirit-anointed one, the Messiah, has arrived. And I am he!"

The response was what you might expect. Happiness and joy. And then they remembered (or at least thought they did) who Jesus was. He had grown up in their midst, they knew his father Joseph, and he did not appear to bring the right messianic credentials to the table. After a few choice words from Jesus, the Nazarenes got so upset that they wanted to throw him off a mountain. Jesus was able to get away from the mob and (wisely) decided to set up headquarters someplace else.

Jesus saw himself as the fulfillment of God's promise to anoint his Servant with the Holy Spirit. Remember our earlier question: What is it that makes Jesus the Christ? The answer is the Holy Spirit. Jesus is the Messiah, the Christ, because of his anointing by and with the Holy Spirit.

I challenge you to read through the Gospels, looking for the power of the Spirit in Jesus's life, and I guarantee you will be amazed. You will wonder why you have never seen the priority role of the Spirit before. Jesus appears to do everything, at least everything of consequence, by and through the Spirit.

Here is a brief summary of all the Bible says that the Spirit did in the life of Christ: Jesus was conceived by the Spirit (Luke 1:34–35); Jesus was predicted and anticipated by the Spirit (Luke 2:25–27); the Spirit was primary at Jesus's baptism (Matt 3:16); Jesus was recognized and identified by the Spirit (John 1:32–33); he was led by the Spirit (Luke 4:1–2); he taught by the Spirit (Luke 4:14–15); he directed through the Spirit (Acts 1:2); he was empowered by the Spirit to do miracles (Matt 12:22–32); he rejoiced in the Spirit (Luke 10:21); he went to the cross by the Spirit (Heb 9:14); and Jesus was raised by the Spirit (Rom 8:11).

It might have been easier to list all the things that Jesus didn't do by the Spirit!

All this brings up another very significant question: Why the Spirit? If Jesus is already fully divine (which we have taken pains to establish), what need would he have of the Holy Spirit? Why add more God to someone who is already completely God?

The answer, of course, is that the Son of God, as God, has no need of the Spirit's power or enablement. But if the Son of God is going to become a man and live his life as a real, honest-to-goodness human, even if he does not give up his divinity, then there is great need.

Go back to Phil 2:5–8. If Paul is correct that Christ Jesus "emptied" himself by adding a human nature, living a real human life as a servant, then the exercise of many divine attributes would be inconsistent with authentic human living. Human nature does not include being omniscient (all-knowing), omnipotent (all-powerful), or omnipresent (being everywhere at all times). Humans are not omni-anything, at least not anything good.

What happened when Jesus took on a human nature and human existence? He "emptied" himself by refusing to exercise those divine attributes that are inconsistent with authentic human existence and his redemptive mission; instead, he continued to submit to God the Father and relied upon the Spirit. The Son of God did not give up the attributes of deity. How could he? He is God Almighty, and he cannot de-God himself (thankfully), even in becoming man. Instead, Jesus chose not to use those attributes that would have rendered his life and experience something more or less than human.

So are advocates of the Green Lantern heresy correct? Was Jesus just a pious, but mere, man whom the Spirit was given to enable him to do all God required? The Adoptionists were correct that Jesus relied upon the Holy Spirit. But they were dead wrong in why he did so. Jesus did not need the Holy Spirit because he was not divine. He relied on the Holy Spirit because he chose to live as an authentic human. And as we will see, in the remainder of this chapter and the next, that makes all the difference in the world.

WHY IS THIS IMPORTANT?

We have already demonstrated that unless Jesus Christ was fully human and fully divine, he could not have saved us. It takes a fully human Jesus to substitute for human sin, and it takes a fully divine Jesus to atone for all sin, once and for all. But there are other aspects of the salvation that Jesus brings that he would not be able to if he were more like Green Lantern than the Jesus of the Bible.

The Spirit-Anointed Man Became the Spirit Giver. There are many things that Jesus came to do. He came to live a sin-less life. He came to reveal God the Father. He came to die. He came to conquer death. Something that is often overlooked but was a huge priority for Jesus is this: Jesus came to send the Holy Spirit.

There is a progression of anticipation throughout the Old Testament that, one day, the Lord would pour out his Spirit on all of his people. In Numbers 11, Moses, in almost wishful fashion, lamented, "If only all the LORD's people were prophets and the LORD would place his Spirit on them!" (v. 29). Later, Moses promised the Israelites that one day, after much failure and misery, "the LORD your God will circumcise your heart and the hearts of your descendants, and you will love him with all your heart and all your soul so that you will live" (Deut 30:6). Eight hundred years later, after the Israelites had gone into exile, the prophet Ezekiel foretold of a time when the Lord would bring forgiveness and a new heart. He would do this by placing his Spirit within them, who would cause them to obey (Ezek 36:25–27). Finally, the Lord promised through the prophet Joel that one day he would pour out his Spirit on all of his people in an unprecedented way (Joel 2:28–29).

So it should come as no surprise that Jesus placed high priority on the work of the Spirit. Remember his conversation with Nicodemus in John 3? Jesus told the Pharisee, "Unless someone is born of water and the Spirit, he cannot enter the kingdom of God" (v. 5). When Nicodemus responded that he did not understand, Jesus was incredulous. "Are you a teacher of Israel and don't know these things?" (v. 10). Jesus essentially said, "Nicodemus, this is basic stuff. How can you not understand?" The hopes and dreams of Israel should have been pinned on the future coming of the Spirit of God. I say "should have" because it is apparent from the Gospels that many of the Israelites did not recognize the importance of the promised coming of the Spirit. Jesus did.

But you and I, at times, are like Nicodemus and the Hebrews, aren't we? We have all, at some point, undervalued the person and work of the Holy Spirit. Just before Jesus was arrested, he gathered with his disciples for the Last Supper and some final instruction. It would be difficult to overstate the stress that the disciples were feeling at this point. Jerusalem was not a safe place for them, and to make matters worse, Jesus had been telling them that he probably would not survive this last trip to the Holy City. Looking in their eyes, he knew that they were having a difficult time processing all that he was saying (see John 16:12) and that he had freaked them out by telling them yet again that he was going away (16:5–6). But he pressed forward and tried to convince them that they were actually better off if he left. "It is for your benefit that I go away" (16:7).

What?

Put yourself in the place of the disciples. They had left everything to follow Jesus. They were convinced he was the Christ, the long-awaited Savior. They were risking their lives, even at that moment, to be with Jesus. And he had the audacity to tell them they would be better off if he left?

Jesus meant it. And he explained why. "Because if I don't go away the Counselor [the Holy Spirit] will not come to you. If I go, I will send him to you" (16:7).

There are two important things to take away from this. First, Jesus tied his going away, that is, his crucifixion (and subsequent resurrection and ascension), with his sending the Spirit. The logic is this: The sending of the Spirit is one of the great promises of the new covenant, but the new covenant can only be initiated with blood—atoning blood. And it cannot be the blood of bulls, goats, or sheep. It has to be blood that will completely and finally atone for human sin. If Jesus does not go to the cross, he cannot send the Spirit. All those Old Testament promises of the coming of the Spirit cannot be fulfilled unless the Spirit-anointed one goes to the cross.

Second, Jesus is the one who sends the Spirit. In other passages, it is the Father (see John 14:16–17, for example), but in this passage, Jesus plays a vital role in the sending of the Spirit. The Spirit-anointed one would become the Spirit-Sender.

I don't know if the disciples believed Jesus. But he was telling them that they would be better off with the Spirit, but not in his presence, than they were being with him, but without the Spirit.

Do you believe this? Do you understand that the same applies to you? Do you realize that, in God's economy, you as a Spirit-indwelt follower of Jesus are in a better place than the disciples were when they were in the same room with him?

Maybe you sometimes think, *I would be a better follower of Jesus if I could have been there with him.* No doubt, it would have been great to see Jesus heal, hear him teach, or watch him command the wind and the waves. But don't kid yourself. Your best bet for faithfully following Jesus is the presence of the Spirit whom he sent. For Jesus, it is more than a best bet. It seals the deal. His sending of the Spirit guarantees that all of his followers will receive all of the blessings of salvation. The apostle Paul said as much to the church in Corinth: "He has also put his seal on us and given us the Spirit in our hearts as a down payment" (2 Cor 1:22; see also Gal 4:4–7; Eph 1:13; 4:30).

No Green-Lantern-like Jesus, a mere man, possessed with the ability of God to do miracles, could have done what Jesus Christ has done for you. There is nothing in the mission of the Green Lantern that involves distributing power to all who are loyal to him. But Jesus does not just give you power. He gives you divine presence. It takes the second person of the Trinity, the true Son of God, to send the third person, the Holy Spirit, to you. An adopted Jesus, who was a mere man given power, would not have the authority or intrinsic ability to give you the Spirit. And the Spirit the Son sends to you is the same Spirit who enabled and empowered his entire ministry.

Don't ever forget what I like to call the "grace of place in redemptive history." It is a wonderful thing to be born on this side of the cross, knowing the full-orbed gospel. It is an even better thing to be sealed and empowered by the Spirit of God at Jesus's behest. The coming of the Spirit was a crazy dream for Moses; it was a distant hope for Ezekiel; but it is true for you.

Jesus Could Not Have Defeated Satan, Evil, and Death If He Were Just a Man. When Jesus went to the cross, he was not merely a victim who was taking on himself a punishment that others deserved. He was also dealing a deathblow to Satan, defanging the prince of darkness, and initiating the demise of the Devil's horrible rule.

One of Jesus's closest friends said exactly this: "The Son of God was revealed for this purpose: to destroy the devil's works" (1 John 3:8). The author of Hebrews explains further: "Now since the children have flesh and blood in common, Jesus also shared in these, so that through his death he might destroy the one holding the power of death—that is, the devil" (2:14). These passages emphasize both the humanity and the deity of Jesus. The defeat of Satan and the destruction of all his evil works could not have been accomplished by a mere human, however empowered by the Spirit. It took more than a Green-Lantern-style hero to save you. It took the incarnate Son of God, in all that he is, to accomplish the defeat, for all time, of our greatest enemy.

I mentioned earlier that when Jesus read the Isaiah 61 prophecy in the synagogue in Nazareth, he stopped in the middle of a sentence, leaving out the part about proclaiming, "the day of our God's vengeance" (v. 2).

But do not think that Jesus decided to leave that part of the prophecy undone. Far from it. Every prophetic word will come true. There will be a day of God's vengeance. One day Jesus will return to take care of all his unfinished business. That day will not be pleasant for the Lord's enemies. Satan is clearly in the crosshairs of God's white-hot wrath, but all those who have persisted in rebellion against God will share the horrific fate of the Devil. And Jesus Christ will be leading the rout.

The death and resurrection of the Anointed One signals the certain end of the Devil's reign. Jesus Christ, empowered by the Spirit, will return in power and majesty. By virtue of his deity, Jesus has all the right stuff to defeat the Devil and his followers. By virtue of his humanity, Jesus has the right to sit on the eternal throne promised to a Son of David millennia ago (2 Sam 7). He will defeat all evil. He will address every wrong. He will balance the scales of justice finally. He will reign forever.

The apostle Paul understood this. He knew that Jesus had to be everything the Bible says in order to do all the Bible says that our Savior must do. That is why, after explaining to the Philippians how Jesus had "emptied" himself by adding humanity and the posture of a servant, culminating in his obedient death on the cross, he burst into praise in his letter:

> For this reason God highly exalted him and gave him the name that is above every name, so that at the name of Jesus every knee will bow—in heaven and on earth and under the earth—and every tongue will confess that Jesus Christ is Lord, to the glory of God the Father. (Phil 2:9–11)

Green Lantern cannot save you. Nor can a Green-Lantern-type Jesus. But the Jesus of the Bible, the divine Son, who is also the Spirit-anointed and Spirit-empowered Christ, certainly can.

DISCUSSION QUESTIONS

QUESTIONS FOR PERSONAL REFLECTION

- How does the Adoptionist's view of Jesus's need for the Holy Spirit differ from the biblical view of his need?

- Are you confident that your Savior is truly greater than Satan? If not, meditate on Col 2:13–15 and consider the triumph of God in Christ.

- Have you ever read through the Gospels looking for the Holy Spirit? Are you surprised at how dependent Jesus was on the Holy Spirit?

- What confidence do you get from realizing that the same Spirit who empowered Jesus is the one he sends to empower and enable you?

QUESTIONS FOR GROUP DISCUSSION

- One of the ways you might fall into the Green Lantern heresy is to think that Jesus died to forgive sins but doesn't have what it takes to fight evil in the world. Why might it be tempting to believe this? What did you learn that combats this lie?

- Do you really believe that Christians today with the Spirit but without the physical presence of Jesus are better off than having the personal presence of Jesus but without the Spirit? Why or why not?

- Of what did Jesus empty himself? Of what did he not? Why is it important that Jesus not exercise omnipresence or omnipotence during his first advent ministry?

- You were given a list of things Jesus did by the Spirit. Which one surprised you and why?

- What difference does it make in your life that Jesus is not like the Green Lantern?

FOR FURTHER STUDY

Read John 14:14–17; 16:7–15; and Acts 1:1–11 and consider the priority of the sending of the Holy Spirit. What kind of presence of God and power of God has Jesus promised to send? What is the Holy Spirit shaping you into? Are you ever at cross-purposes with God in his work of transforming you?

6

THE HULK CAN'T SAVE YOU

| THE PERILS OF APOLLINARIANISM | JESUS HAD A DIVINE MIND IN A HUMAN BODY |

Hah! When Hulk smashes something, it stays smashed!
— *The Defenders* 1, no. 16 (October 1974)

He will not break a bruised reed, and he will not put out a smoldering wick, until he has led justice to victory. The nations will put their hope in his name.
— A messianic prophecy attributed to Jesus Christ (Matthew 12:20–21)

Before I was a theology professor, I was a nuclear engineer. Seriously.

That meant that in college and at work I spent a lot of time working with things that were impossible to see with the naked eye—things like neutrons, alpha particles, and gamma rays.

For a guy schooled in the Marvel Comics universe, gamma rays and nuclear radiation were quite exciting. Almost too exciting. In my labs, when we were supposed to be measuring gamma radiation for the purpose of safety, my mind would occasionally wander to trying to figure out how much gamma radiation it would take to turn someone into the Hulk.[1] (Now you know why I am no longer an engineer.)

The Hulk's alter ego is the enigmatic physicist, Bruce Banner. How Dr. Banner becomes the Hulk varies slightly in the comics, movies, and television shows, but all forms involve Banner taking what should have been a lethal dose of gamma radiation.

In the 1970s television series *The Incredible Hulk*, Dr. Banner, grieving the death of his wife in an auto accident and haunted by his inability to pull her from the wrecked car before she died, discovers that some people are able to summon superhuman strength in high-stress situations. He also finds that high levels of solar gamma radiation are necessary for that extra strength, but tragically, on the day of his wife's death, solar gamma radiation levels were low. Frustrated that he was not able to save her, he intentionally bombarded himself with gamma rays to make up the deficit he'd lacked when his wife's life was on the line. Shortly thereafter, while throwing a fit over a flat tire in a rainstorm, Banner transforms into the Hulk.[2]

From that point, Banner becomes the Hulk whenever he gets angry, and keeping a rein on his temper is a constant problem. The television series saw Banner traveling the nation in search of a cure (or at least a good anger-management counselor).

---

[1] I spent most of my time as an engineer working in front of a computer, so the only radiation that I absorbed came from my computer monitor. That is enough to make you cranky, but not enough to give you superpowers.

[2] In the Marvel comics, Dr. Banner rescued a teenager who had snuck onto a testing range on the day that Banner's gamma bomb was to be detonated. Pushing the teenager into a protective ditch, Banner was not able to save himself, and he was hit with the force of the bomb. Miraculously, Banner survived with little apparent effect. Little effect, that is, until nightfall, when he turned into a grey, monstrous, ... well, hulk. Marvel eventually changed the color from grey to the more familiar green.

He always came up empty on that score, but he never failed to find rage-inducing schemes and crimes. To be fair, Banner usually tries to advise his antagonists not to get him irked, but his warning, "Don't get me angry. You wouldn't like me when I'm angry," is rarely heeded. The result: rage, soon followed by carnage, pain, and overall chaos.

"You wouldn't like me when I'm angry" might be the most understated of all warnings. The Hulk is a humanoid of immense proportions who is largely bent on destruction. Standing almost nine feet tall, the Hulk has a strength that is limited only by his ability to rein in his temper. That is, the angrier he gets, the stronger he gets. He can hop across oceans, move mountains, shift islands, and destroy asteroids with a single punch.

Hulk's strength is matched only by his durability. He is, in a word, indestructible. Armed with regenerative powers, he can endure atomic blasts and lava baths. Nothing can harm him—and if it could, Hulk could restore himself almost immediately. So powerful is Hulk that the military is eager to draft him into its service. Many Hulk comics are dedicated to the adventures surrounding his refusal to accept their "employment offers."[3]

But what Hulk possesses in strength, he lacks in brains. One would think that some of Dr. Banner's intelligence would cross over. One would be wrong. Hulk might be able to lift a *ton*, but he cannot spell it. His intellect and emotional level is childlike . . . small-child-like. Whereas Dr. Banner is a physicist, Hulk communicates in short sentences with monosyllables, and his problem-solving ability is summed up in his favorite phrase, "Hulk smash!"

After a period of mayhem and destruction, the Hulk transforms back, and Bruce Banner usually wakes up in a ditch or

---

[3] To this point, the Hulk remains a conscientious objector to the army's draft plans. He does, however, look good in green.

under cover somewhere. He remembers nothing of what had just previously taken place, but his tattered clothes are strong indicators that nothing good happened the night before. Powerless to control his temper and avoid transformation into the Hulk, Banner does invest in super-stretchy pants so at least he is able to maintain some level of modesty and decorum during and after his time as the monstrous humanoid.

So there is very little of Bruce Banner left when he transforms into the Hulk. He does not possess Banner's intelligence, compassion, or memory. The Hulk is able to do remarkable things, but the attributes that enable such feats are so far beyond those of ordinary humans that he is really no longer human at all. Bruce Banner has essentially been taken over by someone (or something) who is not human.

Many people have the same idea about Jesus. There are those who suggest that Jesus was a man with an ordinary human body but a divine will. The result is a Jesus who is partly human and partly divine. Because deity is greater than humanity, the human aspect of Jesus is soon overwhelmed by the divine, leaving a being who is really not human at all anymore.

I call this kind of thinking the Hulk heresy, but it was around long before anyone made Dr. Banner angry.

THE HERESY

To set the stage, we need a quick refresher on what happened at the First Council of Nicaea. Arius, chief proponent of the Thor heresy, taught that Jesus Christ was a god, but not the God. A man named Athanasius rose up to take on Arius and defend the biblical teaching that unless Jesus was fully God, equal to God the Father in essence, Jesus could not have saved sinners. The Council of Nicaea met and declared that the Father and the Son are *homoousios*, eternally equal in essence and person. We also found that even though the Nicene council condemned Arianism, the issue was far from settled. Even after Nicaea, the church continued to struggle to explain who Jesus actually was.

A friend of Athanasius, named Apollinaris, contributed to the confusion. He suggested a model of Jesus that he thought would bring clarity to the issue, but his proposal was every bit as bad as that of Arius. His idea was so bad, in fact, that he got his own heresy named after him, just like Arius.

In the year 362, Apollinaris was named bishop of the church in Laodicea. You might recall that Laodicea is the site of the church that Jesus castigates in Rev 3:14–22 for being lukewarm and proud. It made Jesus want to puke—literally (see v. 16). Not exactly what you want your church to be known for.

Three hundred years later, the Laodicean church would make another singular contribution to the Christian Hall of Shame when her bishop went off the rails in his own attempt to defeat heresy.

Apollinaris meant well. What he learned from watching his friend Athanasius is that the full deity of Jesus Christ must be protected because nothing less than salvation is at stake. As we learned in our discussion of Liberalism (the Batman heresy) and Arianism (the Thor heresy), if Jesus is not fully divine, then he cannot save anybody. Apollinaris believed this and was zealous to defend the deity of Christ.

Apollinaris understood that a human was composed of three parts: a body, a sensitive soul, and a rational mind. He did not get this from reading his Bible; he actually got it from the Greek philosopher Plato. Apollinaris did notice that Paul ended his first letter to the Thessalonians with this blessing: "Now may the God of peace himself sanctify you completely. And may your whole spirit, soul, and body be kept sound and blameless at the coming of our Lord Jesus Christ" (1 Thess 5:23). Now, I do not think that Paul was trying to tell us that a human is composed of three and only three things. I suspect that Paul was taking some representative aspects of the human and basically saying, "May God bless, save, and keep every bit of you." But Apollinaris found in this verse biblical justification for his platonic anthropology—he believed that Paul had given him biblical warrant to describe the three essential components of a person the way Plato did.

I believe Apollinaris made a mistake that we are all tempted to make. He came to the Bible hoping that it would say what he wanted it to say, rather than seeking to discover what the biblical author wanted to say. The Bible was not written to give authority to our own sensibilities and preconceived notions. It was written because God wanted to make himself known. We must remember that fact; I don't think Apollinaris did.

According to Plato, the body is, well, the body. The sensitive soul is that part of us that animates the body, that makes us alive. We move, breathe, live, sense, and feel through our sensitive soul. The rational mind is the highest part of us, the part that is conscious, that thinks and wills. All three components are necessary in order to be human.

Apollinaris, following Plato, proposed that Jesus was human in that he had a body and a sensitive soul, but his rational mind was divine. The humanity of Jesus was found in his body and life functions. His deity was found in his consciousness, intellect, and decision making. The human rational mind was replaced in Jesus by the divine *Logos* (the eternal Word of God). In other words, the humanity of Jesus contributed the lowest two parts to his being; deity contributed the highest. Jesus was two parts human and one part, the most important part, divine.

This was important to Apollinaris for a couple of reasons. First, he wanted to protect the deity of Jesus Christ. He saw

Jesus Christ as being fully God, and in his proposal, Jesus was the Word, just as John said in the first part of his Gospel.

Second, if Jesus was going to be fully God, he had to be immutable. Today, when we say that God is immutable, we mean that God does not and cannot change in his *person* and *character*. But Apollinaris believed what most did at that time: God has to be *absolutely* unchanging; otherwise he is less than divine. Here is the reasoning: If God could change, then he would go from something good to something either better or something worse. Both of those options are terrible for God. If he changes and gets better, then what was he before? Something less than perfect? And if he changes by getting worse? Well, I don't even want to think about that.

These categories for immutability were rooted in Greek philosophy, but they had made their way into the church. Christians at the time had no category for change that is not for the worse or for the better. God has been, is, and always will be perfect. Any change in God would be either a change toward or away from perfection, and neither option was acceptable. Therefore, God has to be absolutely unchanging in every way.

But if God is immutable (in that way), then what do we do with the incarnation and humanity of Jesus? Apollinaris had no use for a God who suffers, who is tempted, or who experiences emotions. So, he suggested that Jesus Christ was born with a fully formed (divine) mind that was impervious to the kind of change that humans endure or enjoy.

But here is the problem. In trying to protect the deity of Jesus, Apollinaris proposed a Jesus that was really not human. Something that is only two-thirds human is a partial human. This is especially true when the part that is divine overwhelms the parts that are human. In Apollinaris's zeal to protect the deity of Christ, he had basically replaced him with something that looked more like the Hulk, someone whose humanity is overwhelmed and effectively replaced with something more powerful, but decidedly less human. Jesus was basically God in a human shell, impervious to the trials and temptations, joys and sorrows that make up so much of what it means to be human.

Apollinaris sought to defend the deity of Jesus, just like his friend Athanasius. But the church soon recognized that his proposal was as dangerous as that of Arius, just on the opposite side of the spectrum. A series of synods and councils were convened for the express purpose of condemning Apollinarianism, culminating in 381 at the First Council of Constantinople. In addition to updating the Nicene Creed so that it had more to say about the Holy Spirit, a strong statement was made condemning all forms of Arianism (Thor heresy). Apollinaris had to have been excited about that. He was probably less excited when the council condemned Apollinarianism in that same strong statement.

WHO COMMITS THE HULK HERESY TODAY?

Apollinaris died in AD 390, and his bad idea about Jesus largely died with him. I have not met many people who self-identify as Apollinarians. There are no Apollinarian churches, sects, or clubs (as far as I know). But that does not mean that the sensibilities of Apollinarianism do not creep into some Christians' thinking. Some well-meaning Christians who are completely committed to Jesus being both the Son of God, fully divine, and the Son of Man, a true human being, will occasionally lapse into the Hulk heresy. And here is how.

Some Christians think that all God cares about is the "spiritual" part of us and that we relate to God solely through faith. The mind, by their way of thinking, is a hindrance to faith. Study is an impediment to godly living. These people would never pick up a theology book.[4] What they don't realize is that the mind is very important to Jesus. Jesus Christ had a real human mind, and he came to save the mental part of us as well. The renewing of our minds is one of the commands and goals of the Christian life. To ignore or downplay the mind in discipleship is to slip into the Hulk heresy.

I also see people dabbling with the Hulk heresy when I talk to some in churches about fighting temptation. Christians understand that giving in to temptation is a bad idea. Jesus had plenty to say on the subject. He told his disciples to watch and pray that they might not fall into temptation (Matt 26:41). He warned that the one who brought temptation (or "offenses") was in for a harsh judgment (Matt 18:7; Luke 17:1).

But Jesus did not just warn against temptation. He battled it himself. The Gospels of Matthew and Luke record the story of Jesus's battle with the tempter. As we will see, that story, the true account of Jesus's temptation, like everything in the Bible, is there for our benefit.

A Christian is, by definition, a follower of Jesus. Jesus was the perfect example of how we are supposed to live, so we should strive to do what Jesus did, the way Jesus did it (1 Pet 2:21). But when it comes to fighting temptation, sometimes we balk when asked to follow Jesus.

Some well-meaning Christians figure, "Jesus could not *really* be tempted. He was the Son of God." Or, "It's really not a big surprise that Jesus did not sin. He was divine, after all."

Many of the Christians who say such things earnestly believe that Jesus was completely (or at least mostly) human. They know that the Bible says that Jesus was tempted. Some of

---

[4] Of course, I am not describing you. After all, you are reading this fine book on Christology (the study of Jesus Christ).

them even know that the Bible says that Jesus was tempted "in every way as we are" (Heb 4:15).

They just do not really believe it.

According to the thinking of many Christians, Satan might have tried to tempt Jesus. But at the decisive point of temptation, when the trial got really difficult, the divine part of Jesus took control, making him impervious to temptation and Satan's schemes, similar to when, at the moment of crisis, Bruce Banner was taken over by the Hulk, making him impervious to destruction and his adversaries' schemes. Nobody thinks that Bruce Banner, as the Hulk, fought the bad guys as a legitimate human. Likewise, many Christians do not believe that Jesus *really* fought temptation as a legitimate human.

So we cannot follow Jesus's example in fighting temptation. Not really.

If you have ever found yourself thinking this way, then you have unwittingly lapsed into the Hulk heresy. And the results could be devastating. Satan plays for keeps. But Jesus came to save us, to save every part of us, including the manner in which we battle temptation and face trials. He faced and resisted temptation as a man who was fully human. Thus, fighting temptation, the way Jesus fought temptation, is the standard—and it is not an impossible standard.

Following Jesus, the Jesus of the Bible, is actually our only hope. And here is why.

WHAT THE BIBLE SAYS

When we looked at the Superman heresy, we devoted a lot of space to the Bible's clear teaching that Jesus was and is fully human. Among other things we noted . . .

- Jesus had a real human mother and a real human birth.

- Jesus grew up like a normal human child.
- Jesus got hungry, thirsty, and tired like normal humans.
- Jesus died.

Of course, Apollinaris or other advocates of the Hulk heresy would not deny that Jesus was human in those ways. Remember that Apollinaris thought humans are normally made up of a body, a sensitive soul, and a rational mind, but that in Jesus his human mind was replaced by a divine mind. Apollinaris would no doubt say that those proofs that I just listed for Jesus's humanity are all part of having a body and a sensitive soul (that which makes us alive). He could still get hungry, thirsty, or even die, if he had a divine rational mind.

But is it true that a human being is constituted by those three things? And even if a human being has those three things (for the sake of argument), is it true that Jesus did not have a truly human mind? I say no to both questions, because it is not what the Bible teaches.

Humans Are Made Up of Two Main Aspects with Many Different Integrated Parts. The Bible does *not* teach that when God made the first man, Adam was made from nothing. Instead, we are taught that "the LORD God formed the man out of the dust from the ground and breathed the breath of life into his nostrils, and the man became a living being" (Gen 2:7). We are made from two things: Dirt (physical, material) and the breath of life (immaterial). I do not know exactly what the "breath of life" is, but it is interesting that the writer of Genesis gives us these details of the creation of the first man. Though Gen 1:30 indicates that the animals also received the "breath of life," it is only the man and the woman who were made *imago Dei*, in God's image (Gen 1:26–27). And being created in God's image includes material and immaterial aspects. It is fundamental to who and what humans are.

After God had formed the man and breathed life into him, the Bible teaches that man became a "living being." That word translated "being" is the Hebrew word for soul (*nephesh*, if you are into Hebrew words). Literally, Gen 2:7 reads, "the man became a living *soul*." What this means is that humans don't have souls. They *are* souls. To say that we are souls is to say that we are living beings. And the rest of the Bible, both Old Testament and New Testament, uses *soul* in that same way.

"Wait a minute," you might say. "Isn't the soul the part of you that goes to heaven when you die, while the body stays behind in the grave?" According to "Christianese" (the language that Christians, churchgoers, and Precious Moments figurines' salespeople often use), the answer is yes. The immaterial aspect of a human, which Christians often call the soul, does endure beyond death. It is that aspect of the Christian that goes to be with the Lord (see Phil 1:21–24 and 2 Cor 5:8) and awaits the second coming of Christ and the resurrection, when the immaterial part will be given a new body. It is the immaterial aspect of the unbeliever that is banished to Hades awaiting the second coming of Christ and judgment (see Luke 19:22–23; Rev 21:11–15).

But that is not how the Bible uses the word *soul*.

Soul, all through the Bible, describes the person as a created being. Your soul is the totality of your life; it is what makes you alive. In fact, "soul" is often used interchangeably with "life." A soul is a life. Certainly this includes the immaterial aspect of who we are. The soul is your life before God. In many cases, soul also includes the material aspect of what makes you alive, like pulse, brainwaves, and respiratory functions. You might not expect it, because we are so good at speaking Christianese, but *soul* in the New Testament can refer to our natural existence. For example, in 1 Cor 2:14, the "soulish" or "natural" person is the individual who does not have the Spirit—he is a "natural" person. Check out these other verses where the word *soul* is used and judge for yourself: Deut 6:5; 30:6; Judg 5:21; Job 7:11; Ps 57:8; Mark 12:30; John 12:27; and Heb 13:17.

Back in the olden days (a few decades ago), English speakers used "soul" the same way. If there was a plane wreck or ship sunk, the headline might read "250 Souls Lost at Sea!" The headline was not announcing any sort of final judgment verdict on the poor folk who perished, determining whether they would spend eternity in heaven or hell. The writers were simply saying that 250 people had lost their lives.

Back in the really olden days (a couple millennia ago), Paul used the Greek word for "soul" the same way in Acts 27:10 when he warned that if a sea voyage was undertaken, it would result in heavy loss of cargo and souls. Again, Paul was not making a statement of the crew's eternal destiny. He was warning that many would lose their lives if they put out to sea in the storm. And that is why most English versions of the Bible rightly translate the word that way.[5]

You might be thinking, *Didn't Jesus famously warn people not to fear the person who could kill the body only, but to fear the one who can destroy both soul and body in hell?* (Matt 10:28). Yes, but what Jesus was saying is, fear God, who can destroy in judgment the totality of who you are as a created person.

According to the Bible, therefore, a human being is a living being or "living soul" that is composed of material and immaterial aspects. There are many different parts to those aspects. The Bible lists a lot of them. We are composed of bodies (with all sorts of parts), souls, spirits, consciences, minds, hearts, strength, and so on.

---

[5] Just a few of the many Bible versions that translate the Greek word for *soul* as "lives" are the AMP, ASV, BRG, CEB, CJB, CSB, CEV, Darby, KJV, and KJ21.

So what are we to make of all those Bible verses that tell us to love God with all our hearts and souls? I think it would be foolish to think that the Lord has picked out two parts with which he wants us to love him, as though he did not care about the rest. His desires are greater than that.

What he means is that he wants all of us; he wants to be loved with every aspect of who we are.

When Moses commanded the Israelites to love God with "all your heart, with all your soul, and with all your strength" (Deut 6:5), the parts are representative of the whole. Moses used a poetic and (I think) more powerful way of saying, "God wants you to love him with all that you are, every aspect of your being."

It is the same in the New Testament when Jesus instructed, "Love the Lord your God with all your heart, with all your soul, with all your mind, and with all your strength" (Mark 12:30). He was not trying to one-up Moses by adding "mind" to the mix. He was actually doing the same thing Moses did, giving a list of the different parts of a human to represent the whole. Jesus and Moses meant the same thing: love God with everything that you have.

So what is a human? A human is a unified being, composed of material and immaterial aspects with many different parts. And Jesus had all of them, just like you and me. Jesus, like all humans, had a body, a soul, a conscience, a heart, a mind, a spirit, strength, and all the other things that we humans have. This should not surprise us; Jesus was human, after all. And praise God for that.

Apollinaris and other Hulk heresy advocates are wrong when they say that Jesus just had most of the necessary human parts, but lacked a human mind. Such a claim would have been shocking to those who knew Jesus and walked around with him. To them, Jesus knew God as no one they had ever met before.

But he had a human mind. And that made all the difference in the world to them.

Jesus Fought Temptation as a Man, Not a Hulk. The best evidence that Jesus had a human mind is found in the temptation narratives recorded in Matthew 4 and Luke 4. When Jesus battled temptation in the Judean wilderness, he went toe-to-toe with Satan himself. And he did so as a man, more precisely, as a man of God. Here is the story:

> Then Jesus was led up by the Spirit into the wilderness to be tempted by the devil. After he had fasted forty days and forty nights, he was hungry. Then the tempter approached him and said, "If you are the Son of God, tell these stones to become bread."
>
> He answered, "It is written: Man must not live on bread alone but on every word that comes from the mouth of God."
>
> Then the devil took him to the holy city, had him stand on the pinnacle of the temple, and said to him, "If you are the Son of God, throw yourself down. For it is written:
>
> > He will give his angels orders concerning you,
> > and they will support you with their hands
> > so that you will not strike
> > your foot against a stone."
>
> Jesus told him, "It is also written: Do not test the Lord your God."
>
> Again, the devil took him to a very high mountain and showed him all the kingdoms of the world and their splendor. And he said to him, "I will give you all these things if you will fall down and worship me."

Then Jesus told him, "Go away, Satan! For it is written: Worship the Lord your God, and serve only him."

Then the devil left him, and angels came and began to serve him. (Matt 4:1–11)

To set the stage, Jesus was fresh off his baptism by John, where he had been announced as the Son of God and anointed with the Spirit of God for public ministry. Jesus then headed for the wilderness to be tested. Often, when we read the temptation narrative, we want to skip immediately to the part where Satan shows up and the action begins. But the important action began much earlier, in verses 1 and 2.

First off, notice that Jesus was led by the Spirit into the wilderness. The Spirit did not mysteriously disappear after the baptism, only to reappear later in the chapter when the coast was clear. Jesus was directed into the desert by the Spirit, and I take it that the Spirit was there every step that Jesus took.

Second, we are told that Jesus fasted for 40 days and 40 nights. One of the main points to fasting is to say no to your body and a real physical need (hunger) so that you can train the totality of your being (including your mind), in spite of your body's protestations (hunger pangs), to say yes to God. So, when you fast, you say no to food (for a while) and yes to spiritual disciplines, such as prayer and meditation.

Prayer, as you know, is talking to God. Christian meditation is quiet, but intense, reflection on the truths and promises of God. I know that in our culture, when we think of meditation, we think of hippies or exercisers sitting in the lotus position, eyes closed, legs crossed, fingers making the "A-OK" sign, attempting to "empty" their minds by focusing on the sound of one hand clapping (or on how they will get themselves unstuck from the awkward position). That is NOT biblical meditation.

Biblical meditation such as we find in Ps 1:2 is the conscious mulling over of the truths of God. The Hebrew word for meditation is *hagah*, and it literally means "to mutter over." Have you ever been reading something difficult and found yourself reading it out loud so you can better concentrate so as to understand? That is to *hagah*! Far from emptying your mind to "meditate," biblical meditation is to fill your thoughts with the Word of God and work it over in your mind in the way my youngest boy works a hard candy around in his mouth, trying to get every ounce out of it. This is what Jesus was doing for 40 consecutive days before Satan ever arrived on the scene.

When the Devil finally did show up, Jesus had a lot at his disposal: the Spirit of God, prayer, fasting, and meditation. None of those things requires a superhuman, divine mind to employ.

Having read the narrative, you know that Satan came and tempted Jesus in three specific ways. First, Satan suggested that Jesus turn stones into bread to satisfy his hunger. Second, according to Matthew's order, Satan challenged Jesus to throw himself off the pinnacle of the temple to test God's love and protection. And third, the Devil offered Jesus all the kingdoms of the world if he would engage in a little Satan worship. Let's take these one by one.

In the first temptation, Jesus was clearly hungry. He had been fasting for 40 days. Satan suggested that Jesus end his fast by turning rocks into bread. Having been to Israel, I can tell you that the Judean wilderness is one big rock garden. There are millions of rocks, and no one would have missed one or two. What's the harm? But Jesus was submitted to the leading of the Holy Spirit, who had driven him into the wilderness. The fast had been decreed by God, and to end it prematurely by his own initiative would have been to demonstrate a lack of trust in God's goodness and provision.

So Jesus stood up to Satan. But notice what Jesus did not do: he did not laugh at Satan and mock him for not realizing that though he might look like a mere human, he was impervious to temptation by virtue of a divine mind. Far from it.

Instead he did something that appeared very ordinary: He expressed trust and dependence in God by quoting Scripture. He recited Deut 8:3, words spoken by the prophet Moses when the Israelites were in the wilderness to remind them that God had sustained their parents and been faithful. The Israelites were supposed to have learned that "man must not live on bread alone but on every word that comes from the mouth of God" (Matt 4:4).

Jesus believed those divine words, and he would not give in to Satan. Instead, Jesus would depend on God to end the fast, and it would take a word from God to get him to do so. Jesus would wait and trust in God.

So Satan tried again, attempting to test the limits of Jesus's trust in his heavenly Father. The Devil took Jesus to the pinnacle of the temple and dared him to throw himself down. As if to say that two can play the Bible-quoting game, Satan quoted Psalm 91 at Jesus, which promises angelic help to the one who "dwells in the shadow of the Almighty" (v. 1). His diabolical twisting of the Bible must have felt like a taunt: "You say you trust in God, but let's see how much. Throw yourself from this height. God has promised to protect you. Do you believe that? Will God be true to his word to you?"

Jesus, in remarkably ordinary, non-Hulk-like fashion, again turned to the Word of God: "It is also written: Do not test the Lord your God" (Matt 4:7). Jesus was learning to trust in the promises and goodness of God in the difficult times, without a test. There would come a time a few years later when Jesus would have to trust God in the absolute darkest of times when he faced the cross. And trust at that desperate time could afford no test. So Jesus said no to Satan. He would not test his Father.

In an act of seeming desperation, Satan pulled out all the stops and offered Jesus all the splendor and glory of the kingdoms of the world if Jesus would just bow down and worship him. This was a bitter temptation. Satan was offering to Jesus what the Messiah was destined to possess—lordship over all the nations—but Satan was offering it without the sacrifice of the cross. We might wonder if this was even a legitimate offer. Did such things belong to Satan to give?

I suspect that though Satan came by them illegitimately, the offer was at least somewhat genuine. Satan is referred to as the "god of this age" (2 Cor 4:4) and the "ruler of the power of the air" (Eph 2:2). And it is probably significant that Jesus did not question the legitimacy of Satan's offer.

Instead, he commanded the Devil to leave. Do not miss the fact that in the face of temptation, Jesus answered it with another quotation from Scripture: "Go away, Satan! For it is written: Worship the Lord your God, and serve only him" (Matt 4:10).

Jesus did not take the shortcut. He did not violate the Lord by engaging in diabolical and blasphemous worship. The glory of the nations would one day belong to Jesus, but he would take the long and difficult but God-honoring path through the cross. Rule over the nations would one day certainly belong to Jesus, but not at the price Satan was demanding. For that we must be thankful.

But don't miss what follows in the narrative. Look who shows up in verse 11: "And angels came and began to serve him." That angelic help with which Satan had mocked and tempted Jesus, the angelic help that Jesus steadfastly waited upon his Father to send, came. God the Father was true to his word . . . just as Jesus believed he would be. How about that?

Jesus stood up to the schemes and temptations of the Devil and did not give in. He was empowered and enabled by the Holy Spirit. He prayed, fasted, and meditated on the Word of God. And then he brought to bear that Word that was so fresh and so precious to him in his battle with Satan. There is no reason to suppose that Jesus went all Hulk-like, overwhelmed by the divine mind in his moment of crisis, so that Jesus (or what was left of him) was impervious to Satan's arrows. In fact, there is every reason not to do so. Jesus walked into the wilderness a sinless man and walked out of the wilderness a sinless man, with his holiness (and clothes[6]) perfectly intact.

Jesus fought temptation like a man. Just as he bids us to do.

WHY IS THIS IMPORTANT?

Jesus Came to Save Every Aspect of Us, Including Our Minds. Because Jesus was fully human in every way, he is able to save every aspect of who we are. If you are a follower of Jesus, there is not one part of your humanity that he is not able to redeem. That means that it is not just your spirit, the immaterial part of you, that has been saved. Your mind, your strength, your will, your soul, even your body has been redeemed. We would expect this, since, as we have seen, we are commanded to love the Lord with every last part of who we are. So it stands to reason that our destiny is to be able to love the Lord with every last part of who we are. And that includes our minds.

The apostles, in the New Testament, emphasized the role of the mind in the Christian faith. Unbelievers have had their minds blinded, "to keep them from seeing the light of the

---

[6] No Hulk-induced tatters, but it should be noted that 40 days in the Judean wilderness can do a number on designer robes. Special thanks to Joshua Jen for correcting my oversight on such matters.

gospel of the glory of Christ" (2 Cor 4:4). The result is that their "minds are depraved" (1 Tim 6:5) and "defiled" (Titus 1:15). Therefore, Paul warned believers that our minds "may be seduced from a sincere and pure devotion to Christ" (2 Cor 11:3), and he prayed that the "eyes of your heart may be enlightened so you may know what is the hope of his calling" (Eph 1:18). The ongoing work of salvation is described as being "renewed in the spirit of your minds" (Eph 4:23), and the result of an active prayer life is that the "peace of God, which surpasses all understanding, will guard your hearts and minds in Christ Jesus" (Phil 4:7). Peter instructs the Christians to get their "minds ready for action," by setting their "hope completely on the grace to be brought . . . at the revelation of Jesus Christ" (1 Pet 1:13).

The mind matters in the Christian life. So, Jesus had to save it, like every other part of us. And to do so, he had to have a human mind.

The great church father Gregory of Nazianzus (329–389), while taking on Apollinaris himself, said it best: "For that which He has not assumed He has not healed; but that which is united to His Godhead is also saved."[7] Translation: If Jesus did not have it in him, then he did not and could not save it in you.

So if Jesus were human only in body and soul (whatever that means) but had a divine mind, then there would be no reason to suppose that our minds are salvageable, regardless of what Christ did on the cross.

But Christ did have a human mind. And he wants ours submitted to him.

---

[7] Gregory Nazianzen, "Select Letters of Saint Gregory Nazianzen," in Philip Schaff, ed., *A Select Library of Nicene and Post-Nicene Fathers of the Christian Church*, vol. 7, *S. Cyril of Jerusalem, S. Gregory Nazianzen* (New York: Christian Literature, 1894), 440.

The priority of right thinking in the Christian life is enormous. Paul instructed the Corinthian Christians to demolish strongholds, but he was not arguing for an unthinking, Hulk-like Christian who turns his mind off and batters opponents into submission ("Christian smash!"). Rather, he instructed that this was to be accomplished by taking "every thought captive to obey Christ" (2 Cor 10:4–5). I used to think that to obey that command I had to focus on thinking only about the right things—like Paul told the Philippian Christians: "Finally brothers and sisters, whatever is true, whatever is honorable, whatever is just, whatever is pure, whatever is lovely, whatever is commendable . . . dwell on these things" (Phil 4:8). I was supposed to cloister my mind away and only think about "Christian things." But I soon discovered that trying to think about only "Christian things" all the time got boring, then difficult, and finally impossible, especially if I eventually got out of bed in the morning. Now I realize that Paul was asking for something far greater and more important. Followers of Jesus are not to think only about the right things; Jesus wants us to think rightly about everything. That is, he wants us to think about all things the way he thinks about them, no matter the situation or circumstance, whether it be mathematics, changing engine oil, reading about current events, or just doing household chores. He desires that we share his perspective on all things.

So that part of our humanness, our minds, has been redeemed by Christ, and in the last days, that part of our humanness will be perfected. In the meantime, followers of Jesus are to "be transformed by the renewing of your mind" (Rom 12:2), and "set your minds on things above" (Col 3:2). This is to be done the same way Jesus did it—reading and memorization of Scripture, meditation, and prayer. We are to do this so that we can think the way that Jesus does about everything.

Why? Jesus died to save you. He wants all of you, including your mind.

Jesus Is Our Help in Temptation—but How? Every time Jesus fought temptation, the stakes were incredibly high. Because if Satan could cause even the smallest sin in Jesus, all of God's plans for saving his people and reclaiming the cosmos through Jesus would fall like a house of cards. Think of it: all it would have taken was one lustful thought, one proud statement, or one snide remark to ruin all of his Father's plans for redemption. But Jesus did not do any of these things, not even once.

Jesus lived a perfectly sinless life. According to the Bible, Jesus accomplished this, not by appeal to his divine nature or by going all Hulk-like with a divine mind controlling his body.[8] The reason the Bible gives for why Jesus did not actually sin is that he fought temptation.

This should cause us to fall down in wonder at Jesus's feet.

It is a fact that the easiest way to get temptation to stop is to give in. Think about your own life. Have you ever been locked in a difficult struggle over a decision to do something that you know is wrong, but there is a part of you that wants to do it so bad that the fight almost makes you dizzy? The easiest (and worst) thing to do in that situation is to give in. The temptation will immediately cease. Until the next time.

But Jesus never gave in, not even once. At the point where every other man or woman would have given in, Jesus kept fighting and kept fighting and kept fighting. He has faced temptation

---

[8] Many Christians believe that Jesus could not have sinned because he is God and it is impossible for God to sin. I would count myself among that group. But the reason that Jesus *could* not have sinned is different from the reason why Jesus *did* not actually sin. According to the biblical narratives, the reason that Jesus did not sin is because he fought temptation.

to degrees that we will never imagine because, unlike us, he never gave up and sinned.

That makes Jesus worthy of our awe and reverence.

It also qualifies Jesus to help us in our temptation.

Jesus knows exactly what it is like to be tempted. He was "tempted in every way as we are, yet without sin" (Heb 4:15). No matter what you are going through, Jesus understands. He knows the pressures of temptations; he even knows them at a deeper level than you ever will because he kept fighting temptation all the way to the cross.

This should inspire us. The Bible tells us to "consider him who endured such hostility from sinners against himself, so that you won't grow weary and give up" (Heb 12:3). We should want to do better, to live more faithfully, to fight temptation even longer and harder when we remember Jesus. Of course, we are all so fatally flawed as sinful people that inspiration only gets us so far. Thankfully, Jesus is far more helpful than a motivational speaker or life coach.

Jesus takes that knowledge of temptation and puts it to use for you. The Scriptures explain it this way: "For since he himself has suffered when he was tempted, he is able to help those who are tempted" (Heb 2:18).

Jesus not only knows temptation; he also offers help. One of the most encouraging promises in the entire Bible is 1 Cor 10:13: "No temptation has come upon you except what is common to humanity. But God is faithful; he will not allow you to be tempted beyond what you are able, but with the temptation he will also provide a way out so that you may be able to bear it."

In Jesus, we have a great High Priest, the Son of God, who knows exactly what it *feels* like to be tempted. He may not have gone through every exact possible temptation, but he does know and understand every category of temptation. He knows the temptations of wanting to compromise in order to be liked.

He knows what it is like to be lonely. He knows what it is like to have every cell in his body screaming to take a shortcut and not be faithful. He knows what it is like to be in a place where trust and obedience feel impossible. You name it; Jesus has been there. He has the knowledge, the experience, and the resources to get you through whatever it is that you face.

A Hulk-like Jesus would be no help or inspiration in fighting temptation. That kind of Jesus can't save you. But Jesus Christ, the Son of God, who faced and fought every temptation as a man, can.

DISCUSSION QUESTIONS

QUESTIONS FOR PERSONAL REFLECTION

- Do you have a plan for Scripture memory and Bible study? If not, who can help you make a plan and keep you accountable?
- Are you ever embarrassed intellectually to be a Christian? How has this chapter helped you realize that the Lord wants every part of you, including your mind?
- What was the last Christian book that you read to help you follow Jesus (besides this book and the Bible)?
- Do you consciously turn to Jesus when you are being tempted? If not, what might help you remember to do so?

QUESTIONS FOR GROUP DISCUSSION

- Do you think that our preoccupation with cell phones and other screens keeps people from meditating the way the Bible prescribes?
- What are biblical passages you use to help you resist temptation?
- What do your disciplines of reading, memorizing, and praying look like?
- What changes should you make to your spiritual disciplines that will lead you to greater Christlikeness?
- How will the knowledge that Christ overcame temptation help you when you are tempted?
- Discuss temptations and what kind of "way out" God has provided for you.

FOR FURTHER STUDY

Read 2 Cor 10:1–6. Consider the gravity of the circumstances in which we find ourselves in this fallen world. What is the priority of the mind in the battle with the world, the flesh, and the Devil?

7

SPIDER-MAN CAN'T SAVE YOU

THE TYRANNY OF EUTYCHIANISM	JESUS WAS PART MAN AND PART GOD

With my spider-strength, speed, and agility nothing could've stopped me from landing any sports scholarship—or getting on any professional team I wanted. Nothing except a sense of responsibility. And a tiny bit of pride.

—*Amazing Spider-Man*, no. 652 (March 2011)

For even the Son of Man did not come to be served, but to serve, and to give his life as a ransom for many.

—Jesus (Mark 10:45)

My younger boys love spiders. Because of that, a favorite pastime is crawling around in dank and dark places, looking for treasures. A trip under the house is always accompanied by jars and lids, because an arachnid is a great treasure. Spiders are a find more valuable than any precious gem—the bigger and creepier, the better.

I don't like spiders. A spider spotted in my house shifts me into "time to kill" mode. Whenever possible, I avoid dark and dank places, regardless of potential "treasures" to be found. If you ever find me crawling around under my house, it is probably because there is something that needs fixed, like plumbing or electrical wiring, so I am never excited to be there.[1] The threat of Shelob lurking in the shadows does not raise the fun factor. Shelob, for all you non-*Lord of the Rings* fans, is the gigantic evil spider that almost killed Frodo. She left Mordor and now dwells beneath my house. I am sure of it.

My sons even check out and buy books on spiders. Their idea of a good time is spending an afternoon studying the body parts, the webs, and the diets of spiders.[2]

As long as I am not on the menu, I don't care to know what spiders eat.

When I was my sons' age, the only spider I was interested in was the one that bit Peter Parker. Frankly, most of what I knew about spiders I learned from Parker, the alter ego of the "Amazing Spider-Man." Of course, I did not read Spider-Man comic books to learn about the world of insects. But you take the life lessons wherever you can find them.

When Peter Parker was just a child, his parents were killed in an airplane crash. The orphaned Peter went to live with his father's older brother, Ben Parker, and his wife, May. Uncle Ben and Aunt May provided the young orphan with a family, a loving home, and plenty of wisdom.

---

[1] Remember the introduction to the Thor chapter. I am adept at breaking things. Fixing them is another story.

[2] The great philosopher and theologian Jonathan Edwards shared my boys' delight in the study of spiders. That fact gives me a measure of hope for their future.

Peter, into his high school years, was your typical teen-age boy: shy, socially awkward, and afraid of girls. No doubt contributing to his social awkwardness in senior high was the fact that he was a science and photography wiz. His obsession with all-things-geeky led him to a modern science exhibition, where he was bitten by a radioactive spider. When the radioactive spider venom entered the young man, his genetic makeup was altered into something between that of a human and that of a spider. Peter still looked like his young, nerdy self, but his DNA had been forever changed.

Peter soon discovered that he was superstrong, possessing the proportional strength of a spider, able to lift loads that are orders of magnitude greater than his own body weight. He is a human who possesses the agility of a spider, giving him speed and dexterity exceeding that of any human alive.

Peter also felt a tingling sensation whenever danger was imminent. He began to call this his "spidey sense," a warning mechanism that he mastered to avoid troubles of all kinds (except for issues related to his social awkwardness—not even spidey sense could overcome those).

Putting his applied science and physics skills to work, Peter invented a lightweight, but superstrong, "web" substance along with "web shooters" that he attached to his wrists. The shooters enabled Spider-Man to perform the iconic swinging between the skyscrapers of New York City that characterizes the superhero. A suit soon followed, and Spider-Man was born.

But the Spider-Man we all know and love did not really emerge until tragedy struck the Parker household. Given the chance to stop a fleeing thief, Peter uncaringly allowed the bandit to escape, reasoning he was too busy to be bothered. The same thief later mugged and killed his uncle Ben. Robbed of his mentor and stricken by guilt, Peter learned the lesson that serves as the "North Star" for all the Spider-Man adventures: with great power comes great responsibility.[3] From that point, Peter committed himself to fighting crime wherever it occurred.

After graduating from high school, Peter continued his crime-fighting while enrolled in college. Using his technology and photography skills, Peter was able to pay the bills by taking "selfies" of Spider-Man's vigilante work, which he sold to a local newspaper, the *Daily Bugle*.

The enemies that Spider-Man battles comprise one of the best group of villains in the comic book world. Green Goblin, Doctor Octopus, Sandman, Electro, Rhino—what a list! But what makes Spider-Man perhaps the most popular of all the superheroes is not the bad guys he fights externally; it is the demons that he fights internally.

Peter Parker is debilitated by an identity crisis and the doubts that consume him. He does the best he can to keep the streets safe ("just another service provided by your friendly neighborhood Spider-Man"), but he is completely misunderstood by the city. J. Jonah Jameson, editor of the newspaper that employs Peter, is convinced that Spider-Man is a public menace and runs a relentless smear campaign against the web crawler. And it largely works. Very few people trust him.

Perhaps it is for this reason that Spider-Man is so popular with comic book readers.

Spider-Man seems immanently relatable to young readers.[4] He is, after all, the first teenage solo superhero. He is clever and

---

[3] Originally, "with great power comes great responsibility" appeared in a text box in the comics but was retroactively attributed to Uncle Ben. In the movies, the phrase often comes from Uncle Ben's dying words to a grief-stricken Peter.

[4] Spider-Man is so popular with young people that he even had a recurring skit on *The Electric Company*, a PBS show committed to teaching children

a bit of a smart-mouth, with some of the best one-liners in all of comic lore. Peter Parker, though, has no mentors. After his Uncle Ben died, there was no one to advise him. He eventually joined the Avengers, but not until much later in his superhero career. He feels responsible, not just for Uncle Ben's death, but also for the death of his first girlfriend, Gwen Stacy. Peter is alone, afraid to tell anyone that he is Spider-Man, fearing that those who get close to him will be hurt. He is plagued by social awkwardness, self-doubt, and guilt.

Peter Parker seems relatable because he seems so human. But he is not human. Not really.

You see, Peter Parker is not like you and me. He is actually genetically altered, part human and part spider. And someone who is part human and part spider is neither human nor spider. He is a third kind of person, a hybrid of man and arachnid, a Spider-Man.

And many people, trying to explain how Jesus could be both human and divine, make the same mistake. To them, Jesus is a combination of humanity and divinity, a third kind of person, a hybrid of man and God, a "god-man." But someone who is only part human and part divine is neither human nor divine. A hybrid/third kind of person/god-man cannot save us, nor can he do many of the things the Bible says that Jesus did and does for us. This bad idea about Jesus goes by many names, but I call it the Spider-Man heresy, and it has been around for a long time.

THE HERESY

The Spider-Man heresy is usually referred to as either *Eutychianism* or *Monophysitism*. To explain how this bad idea

---

to read. None of Spider-Man's villains ever made an appearance, so I always found the skits disappointing.

rose to the surface, we need to begin with a completely different bad idea about Jesus.

By the fifth century (AD 400s), the church had concluded that Jesus Christ was both human and divine, that he had both a human nature and a divine nature. (Recall that a nature is the essence of a thing—that which makes it what it is.) Affirming that Jesus was a man who was somehow the one God was the easy part. Explaining how that was possible was a little more difficult. Two ecumenical councils met (in Nicaea in 325 and in Constantinople in 381),⁵ but little clarity was achieved. (Fortunately for all of us, it is easier to talk *to* God than talk *about* God.) The question remained: How do the human and divine natures interact, and how are they present in the one person of Jesus?

A man named Nestorius, the bishop of the church in Constantinople, tried to answer this daunting question by maintaining a strict division and separation of the two natures. He proposed a Jesus who not only possessed two natures, but was really two persons with two centers of consciousness in his one body. (I call Nestorius's idea the Gollum heresy. Think of the scenes of Gollum talking to himself—Sméagol—in *The Lord of the Rings* movies for a good visual.⁶) The church did not think much of a split-personality Jesus, so Nestorius's bad idea (named Nestorianism) was condemned as heretical at the Council of Ephesus in 431, and Nestorius was subsequently sacked by the church in Constantinople.⁷

---

⁵ Remember that the "ecumenical" councils were gatherings where leaders from all the churches were supposed to be represented. As we will find, this definition worked better in theory than in practice.

⁶ I almost included a chapter about the Gollum heresy (Nestorianism), but it just didn't fit the superhero theme.

⁷ There is significant doubt that Nestorius actually believed the details of the heresy that bears his name. Significantly, what Nestorius meant by *person*

The Ephesian Council, though, did not put an end to Nestorianism, and its influence was felt for some time, particularly in the short term.[8] Some church leaders and congregants expressed loyalty to the former bishop of Constantinople, while Nestorius himself continued to plead his case for years, believing that he had been misunderstood and misrepresented. But most Christian leaders of the day attempted to distance themselves from Nestorius's "two natures in two persons" proposal.

What often happens in theological disputes is that in one person's zeal to avoid another's extreme error, the opposite extreme is embraced, a sort of theological pendulum. And that is definitely what happened in response to Nestorianism.

Following the Council of Ephesus, a monastery leader (archimandrite) from Alexandria, named Eutyches, traveled to Constantinople in 433 and delivered a series of sermons. In these sermons, Eutyches taught that the man Jesus Christ had one nature (*mia physis* in Greek), not two. That is, after the incarnation, the divine nature and human nature were combined into one. Some call Eutyches's idea *Monophysitism* or *miaphysitism* (from the Greek) because of its emphasis on Jesus possessing only one nature. But most now prefer to call it Eutychianism.[9]

The net result was a single nature in Jesus that was a mixture of humanity and deity. But when you create something by mixing two ingredients, you effectively lose the original two ingredients. We all know that if you mix yellow paint and blue paint, the result is green paint. You cannot get the yellow and blue back, no matter how hard you try. Eutyches wanted to unite the two natures in the person of Jesus, but in his zeal to articulate

---

was not what others thought, but history takes no prisoners, and Nestorius remains the namesake for the heresy.

[8] There are still Nestorian Christians to this day in the Middle East.

[9] This is what happens when you have a bad idea about Jesus.

something that avoided the error of Nestorius, he ultimately denied that Jesus shared a true divine nature with God and a true human nature with humanity. By the time Eutyches was done, Jesus was not human, nor was he God. He was a third kind of being; call him "god-man" with a "god-man" nature. Kind of like Spider-Man.

The church's reaction was swift, but far from helpful. In fact, what followed was one of the biggest scandals in church history. Let me summarize the *low* points briefly: A power-hungry bishop, Dioscorus of Alexandria, found in Eutyches a pawn to be put to service. Dioscorus wanted to elevate the prominence of the church in Alexandria, and when Flavian, the new bishop of Constantinople, spoke out against Eutyches, Dioscorus saw his opportunity.

Dioscorus sided with Eutyches and turned Emperor Theodosius II against his own city's bishop, Flavian, by painting him as a Nestorian. (Think of it as being similar to Spider-Man versus Gollum!) Such a stink was raised that a second council was called by Theodosius II in Ephesus in 449 to settle the issue. Incredibly, Dioscorus was invited to preside over the proceedings (the very epitome of a conflict of interest). More than 100 bishops were invited, but the deck was stacked against Flavian and his contingent, some of whom did not have time to get there (and Eutyches's most vocal and credible critics were not even invited). Add to this the fact that Dioscorus was accompanied everywhere by an intimidating entourage and you have all the makings of an atmosphere not exactly conducive to genuine deliberation and truth-seeking.

Earlier, Flavian had appealed to Leo, the bishop of Rome, for help. Leo responded by writing a letter to Flavian, articulating support and giving a strong theological defense of Flavian's concerns and position. Leo's letter, which came to be known as *Leo's Tome*, proposed a solution to the Christological debate that avoided the errors of Nestorianism and Eutychianism, as well as many of the other heresies we have discussed to this point. Flavian, now armed with the letter from the Roman bishop, hoped to read it in his defense at the synod.

Meanwhile, when the official church representatives (legates) of Leo arrived at Ephesus, their objectivity was challenged because it was discovered they had received hospitality from Flavian on their journey to Ephesus. Since the well was poisoned against the Romans, Flavian was not allowed to read Leo's Tome. Seeing the writing on the wall, the Roman legates decided to leave while they still could, before judgments and anathemas were distributed against them. By the time the council was adjourned, Eutyches was vindicated, a two-nature Christology was condemned, and its advocates, including Flavian, were excommunicated. When Flavian attempted to convene another council to correct the errors of Ephesus II, Dioscorus sent his goon squad to rough him up, and Flavian died a few days later from his injuries. Dioscorus was then able to install one of his guys as the bishop of Constantinople.

Pope Leo was justly incensed over the whole affair. He wrote a letter to the emperor's sister, Pulcheria, blasting the council as a "den of thieves," and so the synod of Ephesus (449) has been known as the "Robber Council" to this day. He also asked Emperor Theodosius II to vacate all the decisions of the synod and that Flavian's murderers be arrested and charged.

To no one's surprise, Theodosius II denied all the requests.

So, if you are keeping score, two of the most powerful churches in Christianity, as well as the emperor, were firmly in the Eutychian camp, and a prominent church bishop had been murdered. Think of it: Most of the church in the East believed the Spider-Man heresy! Things were looking pretty dark.[10]

---

[10] And we are not even to the Dark Ages yet!

But then the emperor was thrown from his horse (literally), and the tide began to turn. Theodosius II died from his injuries. Pulcheria and her husband assumed control of the empire. The new bishop of Constantinople, recognizing which way the political and theological winds were blowing, changed his mind and repudiated Eutychianism. Dioscorus was deposed from his position in Alexandria, and another ecumenical council was called to meet at Chalcedon in 451 (this time giving everyone a chance to attend—no thugs allowed!).

Significantly, Leo's Tome was distributed to the bishops ordered to attend. Its influence was so great that it became the basis for the decisions and writing that came out of the Council of Chalcedon.[11] It was there that Eutychianism was declared to be incompatible with the gospel, the rest of the biblical witness, and Christian orthodoxy. Pope Leo was later nicknamed "Leo the Great," in large part due to his influence at Chalcedon. (It also helped that he later stared down Attila the Hun and saved Rome.) Eutyches is remembered as a heretic, and Dioscorus, who died three years later, is really not remembered at all.

WHO COMMITS THE SPIDER-MAN HERESY TODAY?

Eutyches died in exile, but the heresy that bears his name has survived him to this day. Eutychianism never had much traction in the Western church, where Rome dominated, but a modified version of Monophysitism spread to various parts of the world. Today, Monophysites are found in the Middle East and South India, and Monophysitism is the doctrine of the national churches of Ethiopia and Armenia.

---

[11] This is especially significant because it elevated the reputation of the bishop of Rome, paving the way for his ascendency in the church.

But you don't have to be a card-carrying Eutychian to fall prey to the Spider-Man heresy.

Christians can unknowingly lapse into Eutychian thinking anytime they assume that Jesus Christ was some strange combination of humanity and deity. Maintaining two natures in one person is difficult to explain, so many Christians just blend the two in their understanding. Perhaps Jesus had some humanity and some deity, but he was neither fully human nor fully divine. Thinking that Jesus was some strange mixture of humanity and deity is straight off the pages of the Eutychian playbook.

But the more likely manner in which Christians might lapse into the Spider-Man heresy is much more subtle. It works like this:

Churches are full of Christians who attend worship services on Sunday mornings to sing songs of praise to Jesus Christ. They recognize that his is the name above every name. They testify to his imminent return, when he will judge the world and consummate his kingdom. They know that all that is wrong with the world will one day be made right by Jesus because he has the power, wisdom, and authority to do so. They cannot wait for that day.

But if you were to ask if Jesus understands and knows them, if you were to ask if Jesus makes any difference in their lives today (outside of hope for the afterlife), if you were to ask if they are able to relate to Jesus because Jesus can relate to them, you will probably only get a blank and uncomfortable stare in return. "How could Jesus relate to me?" they might ask. His deity probably overwhelms his humanity the way a drop of ink is overwhelmed by the ocean. And that would be a legitimate train of thought if the natures were combined and blended together (like ink in the ocean).

One of the great ironies of the comic book world is that Spider-Man is often seen as the most relatable superhero. He is seen as the only crusader who knows what it is like to be a teen-ager, the one who can defeat the Green Goblin and later that day be humiliated by the popular kids of his high school. But of course, it is actually impossible for any human being to relate to Peter Parker because he is not like any other human being. The bite from the radioactive spider altered Peter genetically. He has spidey sense, spider abilities, and spider strength. Spider-Man is not merely his alter ego's name; Spider-Man describes what he is.

But Jesus Christ is not like Spider-Man. Jesus is fully and completely human. There is nothing about him that is subhu-man or altered human at all. Of course, Jesus also possesses a full divine nature, but that does not change or diminish his human nature. Jesus is fully human, but not merely human. Everything that makes you a human, Jesus possesses in full, and authenti-cally so.

Yet when push comes to shove, many find Jesus difficult to relate to. He is, after all, God in the flesh. He is the one who died for sins and rose on the third day. He is the one who is King of kings and Lord of lords.

And that makes Jesus a little intimidating, as it should.

But it should not make him less than human, and thus unable to relate to you.

You see, if you have ever wished that you were understood by the one who matters most but despaired that God could ever do so, you have ignored the true and full humanity of Jesus and lapsed into Eutychianism.

If you have ever found yourself unable to pray because the distance between you and God feels too great, and if you have ever felt hopelessly lost because God cannot possibly relate to you (or even if he could, why would he want to?), then you have forgotten that the Son of God became just like you in all of your weakness and humanness in order that he might, among other things, stand as your mediator and advocate before God. You have followed the same bad thinking that has characterized so many who have chosen to walk the path of Monophysitism. In short, you have fallen into the Spider-Man heresy.

The Bible advises a different, and far better, path.

WHAT THE BIBLE SAYS

The Scriptures do not explain exactly how Jesus is both fully human and fully divine. But as we have seen, it affirms these two facts by explicit biblical teaching and by the logic of the gospel. The Jesus that we encounter in the Scriptures was fully human and always fully human, but simultaneously divine and always fully divine. In one favorite Jesus story, recorded in Mark 4:35–41, both humanity and deity are on vivid display.

After a long day of teaching, Jesus decided to sail for the other side of the Sea of Galilee with his disciples. Apparently, Jesus was absolutely exhausted, and he quickly fell asleep in the boat while his disciples assumed the helm for the nighttime trip. Because of the shape of the sea, storms can arise quickly, with winds so high that the small fishing boats of the Galilee would often get swamped. Such a windstorm struck, and the disciples, many of whom were seasoned fishermen, no strangers to the wind and waves, were terrified. They had undoubtedly seen many fierce storms, but they did not think they were going to survive this one. This was no run-of-the-mill squall.

Mark describes it this way: The windstorm was fierce. Waves were breaking over the sides. The boat was being swamped. And Jesus . . . remained asleep.

How fatigued must Jesus have been? This was not a luxury liner or cabin cruiser that Jesus was in. He was sleeping on the floor of a first-century fishing boat, perhaps with a coil of rope for a pillow. Jesus was so tired that he literally could not keep his eyes open. Not even water splashing over the sides of the boat was enough to wake the man. And that is precisely the point: he was a man—human—just like you and me.

But the story doesn't end there. The disciples, fearing for their lives, woke the sleeping Jesus and asked, "Don't you care that we're going to die?" (v. 38). That's an odd question to ask Jesus, but it does demonstrate how scared they were.

Jesus responded by standing and rebuking the wind and waves (the way a parent would rebuke a child): "Silence! Be still!" (v. 39). And to the disciples' amazement, the wind and waves obeyed (unlike what often occurs when a parent rebukes a child). Jesus then asked his friends why they had so little faith, but I don't know that they were listening. They were too awestruck. They wanted Jesus to do something, but when he did do something, they couldn't believe it. I can't blame them; I can see myself reacting the same way.

Their next question was apt: "Who then is this? Even the wind and the sea obey him!" (v. 41). This was clearly no ordinary man. After all, lordship over inanimate creation is not in the job description of most humans. On the contrary, according to the Bible, that kind of lordship belongs to God alone.

Consider Psalm 104, where the psalmist extolls the Lord for being the Creator and enjoying Creator's rights over all that he has made. The Lord "wraps himself in light as if it were a robe, spreading out the sky like a canopy, laying the beams of his palace on the waters above, making the clouds his chariot, walking on the wings of the wind, and *making the winds his messengers*, flames of fire his servants . . . *At your rebuke the water fled; at the sound of your thunder they hurried away* (vv. 2–4, 7, emphasis mine). Directing the wind, ordering the water where to go and when to stop—God is praised for such things because God alone can do them. And yet, didn't Jesus demonstrate that same kind of authority that night on the water?

So we must ask: Which of the following truly character-izes Jesus? The human being who was so weary that he could not stay awake in the middle of a treacherous storm, or the divine being whom the wind and waves obey? Don't we have to answer, "Both!"? Don't we have to say that Jesus is both human and divine?

The question of how deity and humanity intersect in Jesus is not easily answered. Eutyches suggested that Jesus was a strange hybrid of deity and humanity, a bizarre being who walked the earth, kind of human and kind of divine, but in the final analy-sis, not actually human or divine. And the church responded quickly by denying that this could be the case. Despite all the craziness and intrigue surrounding Eutychianism, the church understood that it had to get the answer to this question right. The stakes were (and still are) just too high.

Prompted by the Eutychian challenge, church leaders from the East and West gathered at Chalcedon in 451 and resolved that both full deity and full humanity in Jesus must be affirmed. That is, there was a complete human nature and a complete divine nature—two natures—in the singular person of Jesus.

Following much of the logic and exegesis provided in Leo's Tome, those assembled at Chalcedon were convinced that in the incarnation, the eternal Son of God added to his person a human nature. The Greek word prominently used in this doc-trine is *hypostasis*. It can mean "person" or "defining identity." So the doctrine that Jesus had (and has) two distinct natures united in his one personal subsistence (*hypostasis*) came to be called the "hypostatic union."

How are these human and divine natures combined in the one person of the incarnate Son of God, Jesus Christ? The council was not able to say exactly, but they were able to rule out some alternatives that they judged to be unbiblical and contrary to the logic of the gospel—affirming that only a fully human and fully divine Jesus could save people for God. (Sometimes it is easier to say what something is not rather than to say what something is—this is particularly true of God.) The Chalcedonian council agreed that however the two natures are united, that union is without *confusion, change, separation,* or *division.* These four terms became known as the Chalcedonian Definition, and they have served to this day as boundaries that must not be crossed whenever the church attempts to explain who Jesus is.

The Chalcedonian Definition demands that whatever our proposal for the human and divine natures of Jesus, the natures must be full and completely united in the one person of Jesus without change. They cannot be blended into a third kind of nature (confused or changed). They cannot be split into a part-human/part-divine combination (divided). They cannot maintain their unity by isolating them in different persons (separated). One person, two complete natures.

The biblical evidence is too strong and the implications are too great to deny the doctrine of the hypostatic union. There is no place for Eutychianism (think Spider-Man) if the two natures are united without confusion or change, nor is there any room for Nestorianism (think Gollum/Sméagol) if the two natures are united without separation or division.

WHY IS THIS IMPORTANT?

So, what does it matter if Jesus is more like Spider-Man, part human and part divine, than he is like the Chalcedonian Definition? Why did it matter so much to Christian leaders of the early church, and why should we care today?

We go back to where we started. If Jesus is not everything that the Bible says he is, then he cannot do all that the Bible says he does. And in this case, a Spider-Man-like Jesus might be fun to think about, but not only would he not be able to save us, but he would not be able to provide many of the benefits that come with salvation. And here is why.

Jesus's Resurrection as a Man Guarantees That We Will Be Raised Like Him. When Jesus rose from the dead that first Easter morning, it was the most important event in all of human history. Because of the resurrection, the sins of all those who believe in Jesus are forgiven, and they are justified (declared righteous) before God. It was not enough for Jesus to die for sins; he had to walk out of the tomb as a living human being for sins to be forgiven.

The resurrection demonstrates that Jesus had sufficiently and completely paid the penalty for sins. From beginning to end of the Bible, it is clear that the punishment for sin is death (see Gen 2:17; Rom 6:23). So if Jesus "lies a-mouldering in the grave," still dead, then he is still paying the penalty for sin. And if he is still paying the penalty for your sin, then there is really no basis for your forgiveness. That is why Paul told the Corinthian church, "If Christ has not been raised, your faith is worthless; you are still in your sins" (1 Cor 15:17).

Not only are sins forgiven, but Jesus's resurrection ensures that we will have a resurrection just like his. Jesus provides the blueprint for the resurrection of all his followers by blazing that trail for us. All followers of Jesus can know that they will one day be resurrected because Jesus, the man, was raised first.

Here is how it works.

Adam, everybody's great, great, great . . . grandfather, sinned. We have all read the story in Genesis 3. Whereas, before the tree of knowledge of good and evil episode, there was no sin or guilt, after Adam and Eve ate, there was plenty of guilt and shame. So much so, that it spread to all of their progeny. We are all guilty before God by our position as Adam's heirs, our nature that we inherited from Adam, and our sinful actions.

So we inherited death from our ancestor, the man Adam. We die in sin, just like and because of Adam (we have each added a few sins of our own into the mix as well). But Jesus the man came to reverse Adam's curse. As we saw in chapter 1, Jesus had to be a man to die in our place. But he did not merely die for us. He also rose for us as well. His resurrection, as a man, guarantees our human resurrection.

Paul explained it this way:

> Christ has been raised from the dead, the firstfruits of those who have fallen asleep. For since death came through a man, the resurrection of the dead also comes through a man. For just as in Adam all die, so also in Christ all will be made alive. But each in his own order: Christ, the firstfruits; afterward, at his coming, those who belong to Christ. (1 Cor 15:20–23)

You see, it was not the mere fact of just any old someone rising from the dead that ensures our resurrection. Jesus had to be a man, fully and completely, to bring about our resurrection. A Spider-Man-type Jesus rising from the dead would have been of no benefit to us. But because he was a man, a human just like you and me, we know what our resurrection will be like. It will be just like his.

If you have ever wondered what your ultimate future will be like, you need to know that one day, because of Jesus and only because of Jesus, you will be like him. John said it like this: "Dear friends, we are God's children now, and what we will be has not yet been revealed. We know that when he appears, we will be like him because we will see him as he is. And everyone who has this hope in him purifies himself just as he is pure" (1 John 3:2–3).

What this means is that your destiny is to be like Jesus. John, in his incredible book of Revelation, tells of a future resurrection to life for all who have placed their trust in Jesus (Rev 20:4–5). Eternal life has nothing to do with floating on clouds, playing harps, or looking like a Precious Moments figurine. It has everything to do with an embodied, authentically human existence in a new heaven and a new earth. And that is made possible by Jesus.

If Jesus were some weird hybrid of humanity and deity, like Spider-Man, then his resurrection would not have much significance for our future destiny. He had to be a human to die in our place, and because he was human, our resurrection can be, and will be, like his.

Christian, that is your hope. And John tells us to fix our minds on that future and work toward it. If your destiny is to be like Jesus, then why waste your time and resources pursuing anything other than what leads to that end? Your hope, anchored in the resurrection of Christ, is to be like Jesus. So pursue purity and holiness. Anything else is a waste of your time and dishonoring to God.

Jesus Has Enabled Us to Be Adopted by God, Coheirs with Him. If you have read the resurrection accounts of Jesus in the Gospels, you know that when Jesus rose from the dead, the disciples were overjoyed, but also a bit perplexed. They had no idea of all that Jesus had accomplished, let alone accomplished *for them.*

Jesus hinted at it in his first words after rising (John 20:1–18). We are told that when Mary arrived at the empty tomb after alerting Peter and John, she was too distraught to think straight. Even the presence of angels in the tomb was not enough to overcome her grief-induced disorientation. She turned to see Jesus, but she did not recognize him, so great was her sadness. When Jesus asked her who she was looking for, she could only express her concern that his body had been taken.

Then he called her name: "Mary."

One word. It was not a command, nor was it an explanation. She had probably heard the word muttered, cried, and yelled at her thousands of times. But when Jesus said it, it made all the difference in the world. Because it was Jesus calling her name. She recognized his voice and knew, at that moment, that he was alive. She threw herself at him in joy. But Jesus's next words are critical. "Don't cling to me," he told her, "since I have not yet ascended to the Father. But go to my brothers and tell them that I am ascending to my Father and your Father, to my God and your God" (v. 17).

The risen Jesus Christ identified himself with his friends. He did so with Mary by revealing himself to her first. He did so with the disciples by calling them his brothers. His Father is now also their Father. His God is now their God. His death and resurrection had made it so.

Jesus was saying more than "God is the Father of all living" because he is the Creator of all things. Jesus, the Son of God, has a unique relationship with God the Father that transcends that of the created world. Hebrews 1:2 says of Jesus that "God has appointed him heir of all things and made the universe through him." So when Jesus, with his work on the cross completed, called his followers "brothers" and talked of "my God and your God," he was announcing that he had made possible a different kind of relationship, the adoption of all his followers by God the Father.

Paul explained it to the Galatian Christians this way:

When the time came to completion, God sent his Son, born of a woman, born under the law, to redeem those under the law, so that we might receive adoption as sons. And because you are sons, God sent the Spirit of his Son into our hearts, crying, "*Abba*, Father!" So you

are no longer a slave but a son, and if a son, then God
has made you an heir. (Gal 4:4–7)

Paul used the language of "son," not because he was speaking
only about males. In Gal 3:28, he taught that when it comes
to redemption, in Christ there is no Jew or Gentile, slave or
free, male or female. All, regardless of ethnicity, economic status, or gender, have access to salvation in Christ. The adoption
as "sons" conveys the idea of being a full heir, whether male or
female. Christian, you need to know that God identifies you as
his adopted child, that is, a full heir with Christ. And he identifies himself as your Father.

Do you feel the weight of that? The Creator and Sovereign
Lord of the cosmos wants to be identified as *your Father*. As a
father myself, I understand. I love being the father of my children. It is one of my most precious and cherished self-identifiers.
And that is only a weak approximation to what God feels.

I don't know what the imagery of God as your Father
conveys to you. Perhaps your earthly father was caring and
loving, so seeing God as Father is not troublesome to you.
Perhaps your earthly father abandoned and failed you, so seeing God as Father is difficult. But I know what the imagery is
supposed to mean: You are loved and wanted in God's family.
The triune God—Father, Son, and Spirit—has gone to great
lengths to bring about your adoption. He loves you and is
committed to you.

A Spider-Man-like Jesus, who is a weird mixture of humanity and deity, but neither divine nor human, could hardly establish the basis for your adoption. Perhaps he could have made
more Spider-Man-like beings full heirs along with him, but that
would have done nothing for you and me. You are able to be a
coheir with Jesus because you and he share something vital in
common: humanity.

Jesus Is Our Great High Priest. In the book of Job, the Lord allowed Satan to test Job's faith. The result is that Job went through horrific suffering; most everything that people hold dear was stripped away from him, including family, wealth, and health. A few of his friends showed up to comfort and encourage Job, though most of their counsel turned into accusations. They told Job that he was enduring hardship because he had sinned. God has set the world up to work in a simple cause-and-effect manner: If you are righteous, you are blessed. If you sin, you suffer. But Job could not imagine that he had done anything wrong and sought some sort of audience with God. He believed that if he could only plead his case before the Almighty, then everything would be made right.

But there was a problem. Job was a mortal, and God is, well, God. Job understood that even if he did get an audience, he would not stand a chance. He lamented, "For he is not a man like me, that I can answer him, that we can take each other to court. There is no mediator between us, to lay his hand on both of us" (Job 9:32–33).

Job cried out for a mediator, someone capable of putting his hand on God, someone who knows what it is like to be God, who has the perspective of God. But what was also needed was a mediator who could simultaneously lay his other hand on Job, who knows what it is like to be human, who shared the perspective of Job. Such a being would be of infinite worth to Job in approaching the throne of God and pleading his case for him. For Job, though, that person was not there.

But that person is there for you. Jesus Christ is exactly such a being. The apostle Paul encouraged Timothy with this very fact: "For there is one God and one mediator between God and humanity, the man Christ Jesus, who gave himself as a ransom for all, a testimony at the proper time" (1 Tim 2:5–6). Jesus, and

Jesus alone, has the proper natures to serve in such a magnificent and majestic role. Fully human and fully divine, he can relate *by nature* to both you and God the Father.

Perhaps you do not think that God is able to understand the heartaches that attend being a broken person living in this broken world full of other broken people. But we must remember this:

> During his earthly life, he (Jesus) offered prayers and appeals with loud cries and tears to the one who was able to save him from death, and he was heard because of his reverence. Although he was the Son, he learned obedience from what he suffered. After he was perfected, he became the source of eternal salvation for all who obey him, and he was declared by God a high priest according to the order of Melchizedek. (Heb 5:7–10)

You might be tempted to think, like Job, that your situation is hopeless because there is no one who understands your frailty, and therefore no one who can and will effectively plead your case before the Lord. But we must remember that "he is able to save completely those who come to God through him, since he always lives to intercede for them" (Heb 7:25).

Christ is our Intercessor, our Mediator, our Redeemer, and our Advocate. But he is also our inspiration. When trials feel like they are growing beyond our ability to endure, we are told to "consider him who endured such hostility from sinners against himself, so that you won't grow weary and give up" (Heb 12:3). This counsel would be a cruel joke if Jesus were not like us. If Jesus were some Spider-Man-like hybrid of deity and humanity, what good could it possibly do to consider the suffering of Jesus? How would such a being's endurance encourage us to persevere?

Of course, the man who inspires our endurance is also the
God who enables that endurance. He is the Son of God, who
sent his divine Spirit to empower us. Paul could truly say, "I
am able to do all things through him who strengthens me" (Phil
4:13). Jesus can do that because he is all that the Bible says he is.

Spider-Man cannot save you. A Spider-Man-like Jesus cannot save you either, nor would he be able to relate to you. Only
Jesus Christ, the one who is truly God and truly human, can be
your great High Priest, can sympathize with you in your weak-
nesses, can share his inheritance with you, and can go before
you in resurrection life.

Only Jesus can save you.

Discussion Questions

Questions for Personal Reflection

- Do you ever struggle with the idea that God is your Father? If so, why? How do you think this reality should affect the life of a Christian in daily living situations?

- How would you evaluate your prayer life? Do you need to pray more? Better? More biblically? How should a follower of Jesus pray?

- Does God seem distant and unapproachable to you, not because he is holy and powerful, but because he does not seem relatable? Does it help knowing that the Jesus who is both human and divine serves as your mediator?

Questions for Group Discussion

- Throughout this book, we have covered a lot of church history. Sometimes there has been a significant intersection between church history and secular civil history. What is your response to these major scenes in church politics? Is it discouraging to read about all the maneuvering going on?

- Are you ever tempted to think of Jesus as not really being human? Why?

- Have you ever been in a situation where you didn't think Jesus could possibly understand what you were going through? Did you turn to him for help, or try to do it on your own? What was the outcome?

- In what ways do Christians tend to waste their time and resources on things that don't matter in the end? How would focusing on the hope of becoming like Christ change how you live?

- When you begin to pray, you can know that the Mediator who knows what you are going through, is there in God's throne room. What difference will that make in your prayer life?
- Do you ever struggle with prayer, wondering whether anyone is listening? How can the truth that Jesus is your great High Priest change that?

FOR FURTHER STUDY

Meditate on Heb 5:7–10 and consider how Jesus Christ, though the divine Son of God, could "learn" obedience through suffering. How does the fact that Jesus suffered make him more relatable and more qualified to serve as your great High Priest? What does it mean that Jesus's prayers were "heard because of his reverence"? What do you see in Jesus's prayer life that needs to become a part of your prayer life?

LAST WORDS

Our journey has taken us through two comic book universes, seven superheroes, at least as many bad ideas about Jesus, too many heretics to count, 2,000 years of church history, and an investigation into the most complex issues in Christian theology: the theology of the Trinity and the person of Jesus Christ.

I started the book by making the case that many of the bad ideas about Jesus are embodied in comic superheroes. I find the analogies to be helpful because they teach us two very significant truths about Jesus.

First, no one, real or imagined, compares to Jesus Christ. It stands to reason, therefore, that the salvation that Jesus offers is better than anyone else can offer, real or imagined.

We all need and want a Savior—a hero who will deliver us. I believe this is why the superhero comics, movies, and television shows are so popular. There is something inside each one of us that yearns for a champion to rise up and deliver us.

Second, Jesus is only able to do all the things that the Bible says he does because he is everything that the Bible says he is. This is the way things always work: What a thing *is* determines what it *does*. We saw this over and over. The bad ideas about

Jesus simply cannot deliver all of the things that the Bible says Jesus did and does.

We saw that the Bible testifies to the full humanity and full deity of Jesus. We also saw that Jesus had to possess true and authentic human and divine natures in order to fulfill biblical prophecy, save a people for God, and then see that people through to the new heavens and new earth. No run-of-the-mill savior could do all that—not the greatest of real human heroes, not even the best creations of our most imaginative comic writers.

The person and work of Jesus are so good they have to be true.

Unlike Superman, Jesus, the Son of God, did not just seem to be human. Jesus actually is human in every respect that it takes to be authentically human.

Unlike Batman, Jesus, the Son of Man, is more than a remarkable human. He is in fact fully God, sharing the divine essence equally and eternally with God the Father and the Holy Spirit.

Unlike Hank Pym, and his alter egos, Ant-Man, Giant-Man, and Yellowjacket, God exists simultaneously as Father, Son, and Holy Spirit, the three coequal and coeternal members of the Trinity. Jesus could and did interact with both the Father and the Holy Spirit.

Unlike Thor, a god but inferior to his father, Jesus Christ, the Son of God, is not just *a* god. He is fully equal to God the Father. All that it takes to be God is found in the person of Jesus Christ.

Unlike Green Lantern, a mere man empowered by a ring, Jesus Christ is not a mere man empowered by the Holy Spirit. Jesus depended on the Holy Spirit throughout his life and ministry, but it was not because of anything he lacked in and of himself. The Son possesses all the attributes of deity, fully and completely; he always has and always will.

Unlike Bruce Banner, who is overwhelmed by the Hulk upon transformation, Jesus Christ at all times possesses all that it takes to make him authentically human, and his divine nature does not overwhelm or trivialize any of those essential human attributes.

And unlike Spider-Man, who is a bizarre combination of human and spider, Jesus Christ has a divine nature and a human nature, not a weird hybrid of the two. His humanity is not mixed into his deity.

Because Jesus Christ *is* all these things, we have found that he is able to reign as King of kings, save us from sin, pioneer our resurrection, serve as our example and help in temptation, be our great High Priest, establish us as his coheirs, and much, much more.

The last chapter ended with a church council in Chalcedon. The Chalcedonian council looms large in church history because it established the boundaries for thinking about Jesus that have guided the church ever since.

Meeting in 451 in Chalcedon, near the Black Sea in modern-day Turkey, church leaders, guided by the writing of Leo, bishop of Rome, formulated the Chalcedonian Creed. On inspection, we find that the council was intentional in addressing each of the bad ideas about Jesus that we have considered. Though they did not name the heresies, their language was very specific in countering the claims of each.

It is worth quoting it in its entirety with some commentary.

> We, then, following the holy Fathers, all with one con-
> sent, teach men to confess one and the same Son, our
> Lord Jesus Christ, the same perfect in Godhead and
> also perfect in manhood; truly God *[not a mere man
> like Batman—no liberal Christianity Jesus]* and truly
> man *[did not just seem to be man like Superman—no*

Docetism], of a reasonable soul and body *[completely
human, unlike Hulk—no Apollinarianism]*; consub-
stantial with us according to the manhood; in all things
like unto us, without sin; begotten before all ages of the
Father according to the Godhead *[not a god, like Thor,
but* the *God, equal to the Father—no Arianism; not a
costume of God, like Ant-Man, but coexistent with the
Father through all of time—no modalism; not adopted
by the Father, like Green Lantern, but the true and
equal Son—no Adoptionism]*, and in these latter days,
for us and for our salvation, born of the virgin Mary, the
mother of God, according to the manhood; one and the
same Christ, Son, Lord, Only-begotten, to be acknowl-
edged in two natures, inconfusedly, unchangeably, indi-
visibly, inseparably; the distinction of natures being
by no means taken away by the union, but rather the
property of each nature being preserved *[not a hybrid
nature, like Spider-Man—no Eutychianism]*, and con-
curring in one Person and one Subsistence, not parted
or divided into two persons *[not two persons in one
body, like Gollum—no Nestorianism]*, but one and the
same Son, and only begotten, God the Word, the Lord
Jesus Christ, as the prophets from the beginning have
declared concerning him, and the Lord Jesus Christ
himself taught us, and the Creed of the holy Fathers has
handed down to us.[1]

The Jesus of the Bible is all that the creed says he is, but of
course the Bible says much more. The Gospels are full of stories

---

[1] Christian Apologetics and Research Ministry, "Chalcedonian Creed
(A.D. 451)," accessed December 19, 2017, https://carm.org/christianity/
creeds-and-confessions/chalcedonian-creed-451-ad.

that demonstrate the excellence and wonder of Jesus. But even they do not tell the whole story of the majesty of Christ. At the end of his Gospel, John taunted us with what I find to be the most frustrating verse in the entire Bible: "Jesus performed many other signs in the presence of his disciples that are not written in this book" (John 20:30). Come on, John! I want to know everything about Jesus that I can!

But I understand what John was saying. He didn't have the time or space to recount every Jesus story. He was on a mission to get people to believe that Jesus is all that he actually is and did all that he actually did. That is why in the next verse he wrote, "But these are written so that you may believe that Jesus is the Messiah, the Son of God, and that by believing you may have life in his name" (John 20:31).

In fact, even if he'd had the time, John would not have been able to scratch the surface of the glory of his Lord and Savior. How could he? As John tells us, if all that Jesus did "were written down, I suppose not even the world itself could contain the books that would be written" (John 21:25).

What this means is that your life in Christ is going to be a wondrous discovery of all that Jesus is and does. It starts at your conversion and will continue throughout all of eternity. And here is the great part: You will never grow bored with Jesus. We will have all of eternity (a very long time) to learn of our great God and King, and we will never plumb the depths of his majesty. As we learn and experience more of him, our appetite and capacity to know Christ will grow and grow. We will never lose our excitement because he will never grow familiar. Jesus is all that.

If that is your destiny, then get started now.

Seek Christ.

Pursue Christ.

Meditate on Christ.

Follow Christ.
Live Christ.
Share Christ.
Worship Christ.
Emulate Christ.
Depend on Christ.
Give to Christ.
Live for Christ.
And, if necessary, die for Christ.

And if that is not your destiny because you have never believed the gospel, what is holding you back? After all, superheroes cannot save you. But Jesus Christ, the Jesus . . .

- who is God-incarnate;
- who was born, lived, and taught;
- who was crucified, rose from the dead, and ascended to the right hand of the Father;
- who intercedes for and serves as the great High Priest of his people;
- who will return again to conquer Satan, judge the living and the dead, and re-create the cosmos;
- who will reign forever as King of kings and Lord of lords . . .

In short, the Jesus who is everything that the Bible says he is— *that* Jesus can save you.

EPILOGUE: UNFINISHED BUSINESS

*P*erhaps, as you have read this book, you have come to see that the Bible's testimony about you is true: Left to your own devices, you stand alienated from God and in need of a Savior, someone to save you from sin and the judgment of God that sin inevitably will bring. Perhaps you have become convinced that Jesus is exactly who the Bible says that he is, the one uniquely qualified to be your Savior. If you do not understand yourself to be a Christian, but need and want Jesus to save you, then the time is now.

When a convicted Pentecost crowd asked Peter, who had just preached the death and resurrection of Jesus, "What should we do?" Peter's answer was, "Repent and be baptized, each of you in the name of Jesus Christ for the forgiveness of your sins" (Acts 2:37–38). When a distraught Philippian jailor asked the apostle Paul, "What must I do to be saved?" Paul's response was simple and direct: "Believe in the Lord Jesus, and you will be saved" (Acts 16:30–31). Elsewhere, in a letter to the church in Rome, Paul gave more direction: "If you confess with your mouth, 'Jesus is Lord,' and believe in your heart that God raised him from the dead, you will be saved" (Rom 10:9).

Those are the necessary steps to becoming a Christian. Repent and believe, confess and believe.

The Scriptures do not prescribe a prayer or instruct you to "ask Jesus into your heart." Instead, the Bible uses verbs like "follow," "receive," and "believe." But many people will pray in order to make formal their initial steps of repenting, confessing, and believing. Prayer is simply talking to God and there is no better way to begin the Christian life.

- Confess to the Lord that you are a sinner, one who has rebelled against God and stands separated from God because of your thoughts, words, and actions.
- Call on the Lord to save you. Tell him that you believe that Jesus is who the Bible says he is and Jesus did what the Bible says he did. Confess that Jesus Christ is Lord, that he died for your sins, in your place, and that he was raised from the dead.

God's Word tells us that those "who believe in the name of the Son of God . . . may know that [they] have eternal life" (1 John 5:13). If you believe the gospel then you have been saved to follow Christ. For the follower of Christ, repenting, confessing, and believing are not one-time things. To follow Christ is to embark on a lifetime of repenting, confessing, and believing. This cannot be done alone, nor was it ever meant to be done alone. It is essential that you find a local church where the gospel is preached, where you can grow as a follower of Jesus Christ.[1]

As you embark on this new journey to follow the Lord Jesus Christ, my prayer for you is that you would find in him, the one by whom, through whom, and for whom you were created, the fulfillment of all your deepest desires (Col 1:15–20).

---

[1] If you have no idea how to find such a church, you might find some help here: http://churches.thegospelcoalition.org/ or https://www.9marks.org/church-search/.

SCRIPTURE INDEX

Genesis
1 *15, 25*
1:1 *24, 42, 85*
1:26–27 *133*
1:30 *133*
2 *25*
2:7 *133–134*
2:17 *167*
3 *25, 167*
3:15 *25*
4 *26*
5 *26*
5:5 *26*
5:8 *26*
5:11 *26*
49 *47*

Exodus
3:14 *40*
20:5 *44*
30 *110*

Leviticus
24:16 *40*

Numbers
11 *115*
11:29 *115*

Deuteronomy
6:5 *135–136*
8:3 *140*
29:29 *63*
30:6 *115, 135*

Judges
5:21 *135*

1 Samuel
10 *110*
16 *110*
24:6 *111*
26:9 *111*

2 Samuel
1:14 *111*
7 *47, 119*
7:1–2 *19*
7:12–13 *19*

1 Kings
19 *110*

Job
7:11 *135*
9:32–33 *172*

Psalms

1:2 *139*
3:8 *26*
57:8 *135*
89:27 *89*
91 *140*
91:1 *140*
104 *164*
104:2–4 *164*
104:7 *164*

Isaiah

7:14 *20, 38*
9:6 *20*
9:6–7 *38*
11:1–5 *111*
42:1–9 *111*
43:11 *49*
45:5 *57*
48:11 *44*
61 *112, 119*
61:1–2 *112*
61:2 *119*

Ezekiel

2–4 *39*
36:25–27 *116*

Daniel

7:13 *20, 39*
7:14 *39*

Joel

2:28–29 *116*

Jonah

2:9 *26, 49*

Micah

5:2–3 *20*
5:4 *20*

Malachi

4:5 *64*

Matthew

1:23 *20*
2:11 *45*
3:5–12 *63*
3:11–12 *63*
3:13–17 *58, 63*
3:14 *63*
3:15 *63*
3:16 *64, 113*
3:17 *65, 102*
4 *23, 137*
4:1–2 *138*
4:1–11 *138*
4:2 *23*
4:4 *140*
4:7 *140*
4:10 *141*
4:11 *141*
5:17 *44*
5–7 *57*
6:5–6 *67*
6:9 *67*
7:11 *67*
8:20 *39*
8:21–27 *23*
10:28 *135*
11:14 *64*
11:25 *67*
12:20–21 *123*
12:22–32 *113*
14:22–36 *52*
14:33 *45, 52*
16:18 *93*
18:7 *131*
19:28 *39*
24:30 *39*
24:44 *39*
26:36–42 *65*
26:37 *66*
26:39 *66*

26:39–43 *67*
26:41 *131*
26:53 *67*
27:46 *70*
28:9 *45*

Mark

1:15 *72*
2:1–12 *42*
2:28 *39*
4:35–41 *163*
4:38 *164*
4:39 *164*
4:41 *164*
10:45 *151*
12:30 *135–136*
14:36 *67*

Luke

1:31–33 *9*
1:34–35 *113*
2:4–7 *21*
2:8–14 *45*
2:8–19 *22*
2:25–27 *113*
2:52 *22*
4 *137*
4:1–2 *113*
4:14–15 *113*
4:16–37 *112*
4:20 *112*
4:21 *112*
5:24 *39*
9:23 *37*
10:21 *67, 113*
11:2 *67*
11:11–13 *67*
17:1 *131*
19:22–23 *134*
23:46 *70*

John

1 *85*
1:1 *75, 86*
1:1–4 *40, 58, 85, 88*
1:3 *87*
1:14 *80, 85*
1:32–33 *113*
1:32–34 *64*
1:51 *39*
3 *116*
3:5 *116*
3:10 *116*
3:16 *80, 87–88*
4:1–44 *23*
4:6 *23*
4:6–7 *28*
4:7 *23*
4:23–24 *23*
4:24 *15*
5:19–29 *40, 58*
6:38 *70*
8:54–59 *40*
8:58 *40*
9:38 *45*
12:27 *135*
12:27–28 *67*
14:3 *68*
14:6 *29*
14:9 *51*
14:14–17 *122*
14:16 *67*
14:16–17 *117*
14–16 *68*
15:16 *68*
16:5–6 *116*
16:7 *116–117*
16:7–15 *122*
16:12 *116*
16:23 *68*
16:23–26 *67*
16:24 *68*

16:26 *68*
17:1–25 *67*
17:2 *45*
17:5 *40, 45, 58, 95*
17:10 *45*
17:24 *45*
20:1–18 *169*
20:17 *170*
20:28 *40*
20:29 *40*
20:30 *181*
20:31 *181*
21:7 *84*
21:20 *84*
21:25 *181*

Acts
1:1–11 *122*
1:2 *113*
2:37–38 *183*
2:38 *68*
3:6 *68*
5:3–4 *58*
7:56 *39*
7:56–59 *69*
9:1–19 *92*
9:4 *92*
9:5 *69, 92*
9:27 *68*
10:38 *70, 97*
12:23–24 *44, 47*
13:2 *58*
16:18 *68*
16:30–31 *183*
27:10 *135*

Romans
1:7 *58*
3:23–26 *70*
6:23 *167*
8:11 *113*
8:26 *68*
10:9 *183*
12:2 *144*

1 Corinthians
2:14 *134*
8:4 *57*
10:1–4 *41*
10:13 *146*
12:11 *58*
15:17 *167*
15:20–23 *168*
15:35–49 *15*

2 Corinthians
1:22 *118*
4:4 *141, 143*
5:8 *134*
10:1–6 *149*
10:4–5 *144*
11:3 *143*
12:7–8 *69*

Galatians
1:1 *58*
3:28 *171*
4:4 *72*
4:4–7 *118, 171*

Ephesians
1:3–14 *74*
1:13 *118*
1:18 *143*
1:20–23 *92*
2:1 *49*
2:2 *141*
2:3 *49*
3:14–21 *67*
4:23 *143*
4:30 *118*
5:20 *68*
5:23 *95*
6:18 *68*

Philippians
1:21–24 *134*
2:5–6 *41, 58*
2:5–8 *107, 114*

2:9–11 *120*
4:7 *143*
4:8 *144*
4:13 *174*

Colossians
1:3 *67*
1:12 *67*
1:15 *51, 80, 87, 89*
1:15–20 *51, 91, 184*
1:16 *8, 42, 51, 89*
1:17 *93*
1:17–20 *91*
1:18 *92*
1:19 *51*
1:20 *51*
2:13–15 *121*
3:2 *144*
3:17 *67*

1 Thessalonians
5:23 *128*

1 Timothy
2:5–6 *172*
2:6 *72*
6:5 *143*

Titus
1:15 *143*

Hebrews
1:1–4 *96*
1:2 *41, 170*
1:2–3 *58*
1:3 *41*
1:5 *80*
1:8 *41*
2:11 *58*
2:14 *119*
2:18 *146*
4:14–16 *68*
4:15 *132, 146*
5:7–10 *173, 176*

7:25 *173*
9:14 *113*
10:4 *72*
11:17 *88*
12:3 *146, 173*
13:8 *53*
13:17 *135*

James
1:27 *58*
2:1 *41*

1 Peter
1:13 *143*
1:17 *58*
1:18–21 *50*
1:20 *41, 50*
1:21 *50*
2:21 *17, 131*

1 John
1:1–3 *14, 28*
3:2–3 *168*
3:8 *119*
5:13 *184*

Jude
5 *41*

Revelation
3:14–22 *127*
3:16 *127*
4 *45*
5 *58*
5:1 *46*
5:3 *46*
5:4 *47*
5:5 *47*
5:6 *47*
5:7 *47*
5:8 *47*
5:9–12 *47*
20:4–5 *169*
21:11–15 *134*

SUBJECT INDEX

A

Adam and Eve, 15, 24–25, 108, 167
Adoption, 77, 102, 110, 169–171, 180
Adoptionism, 101–103
Alexander, Bishop of Alexandria, 78–80, 82
Ananias and Sapphira, 58
angels, 9, 21, 45, 52, 137–138, 141, 169
Apollinarianism, 130
Apollinaris, 127–130, 133, 136, 143
Arianism, 78–82
Arius, 78–83, 88, 126–127, 130
Artemon, 103
Athanasius, 78–79, 82, 126–127, 130
Atonement
    Example Theory, 33
    Penal Substitution, 33

B

baptism of the Spirit, 63

C

Caesar Augustus, 21
Callistus, 59
Cerinthus, 14

Chalcedonian Creed, 179–180
Chalcedonian definition, 166
Christian Liberalism, 33–36, 105
Christmas, 20–21
Constantine, 80–82
Council of Chalcedon, 160, 165–166, 179
Council of Constantinople, 130, 156
Council of Ephesus, 156–157
Council of Nicaea, 80, 126–127, 156
crucifixion, 24, 117

D

David, 19, 47, 110–111
Davidic covenant, 19
Day of Atonement, 26
day of the Lord, 64, 111
Dioscorus, 158–160
Docetism, 6, 13–15
dynamic monarchianism, 101

E

Ebionism, 103
eternal life, 14, 169, 184
Eutyches, 157–160, 165
Eutychianism, 155, 157, 159, 160, 162, 165–166

F

fasting, 23, 138–139
Flavian, 158–159
forgiveness, 8, 43–44, 69, 71, 104, 115, 167, 183

G

Gethsemane, 45, 65–66
Gnosticism, 14–15
God the Creator, 85–87, 89–90
Gollum, 156, 158, 166
Gospel, xi, 2, 6, 8, 12, 18, 20, 22–23, 24, 27, 34–35, 37–38, 48, 50, 59, 62, 67, 70, 72, 84, 88, 102, 113, 116, 118, 129, 143, 160, 163, 165, 169, 180, 182, 184
Gospel of Thomas, 22
Greco-Roman philosophy, 13, 15
Gregory of Nazianzus, 143

H

heaven, 24, 42, 45–46, 51, 58, 64, 65–66, 70, 81, 89, 91, 94, 102, 107, 120, 134–135, 169
homoousios, 81–82, 127
hypostasis, 165
human composition, 127–130
hypostatic union, 165–166

I

imago Dei, 15, 133
Immanuel, 20, 27, 38
immutability, 129
incarnation, 14, 27, 32, 34, 95, 102–103, 110, 129, 157, 165

J

Jehovah's Witnesses, 83, 86, 89
Jerome, 82
Jesus
    accepts worship, 44–45
    baptism, 58, 64–65, 102, 113, 138
    birth, 18, 20–22, 40–41, 45, 111
    conception, 20–21, 108
    defeated Satan, 118–119
    deity, 7, 13, 16, 36, 37–40, 41, 44, 48, 58, 82, 84, 106–107, 114, 119, 126, 128, 157, 161, 163, 165, 169, 171, 173, 178
    dependence on the Holy Spirit, 70, 110, 114, 178
    head of the Church, 92–93
    High Priest, 8, 68, 84, 146, 172, 174, 176, 179, 182
    humanity, 7, 12–15, 18, 20, 24, 28, 50, 106, 108–109, 119–120, 126, 128–129, 133, 142, 155, 157, 158, 161–163, 165, 169, 171–173, 178
    Lion of Judah, 47
    sends the Spirit, 115, 117–118
    sinlessness, 50, 115, 142, 145
    Son of David, 19, 27, 38, 110, 119
    Son of God, 13–14, 16, 18, 27, 42, 62, 64, 68, 71, 78, 81, 83, 86, 88–89, 94–95, 102, 104, 106, 107–108, 110, 114, 118–119, 130–131, 137–138, 146–147, 162, 165, 170, 174, 176, 178, 181
Jesus Seminar, 34–36
John the Baptist, 63
Judaism, 15

K

kenosis, 107–110
Kingdom of God, 12, 48, 63, 82, 116

L

Last Supper, 116
Leo, 158–160, 179
Leo's Tome, 158–160, 165
Lord's Supper, 62

M

meditation, 62, 138–139, 144
mind, 136–137, 142–144
miracles, 32, 41, 48, 105, 113,
    118
Modalism, 57, 61, 62
monogenes, 88
Monophysitism (see also
    Eutychianism), 155, 157, 160,
    163

N

Nathan, 19, 47
Naturalism, 16
Nestorianism, 156–157, 159, 166
Nestorius, 156–157, 158
New Covenant, 42, 117
New World Translation, 86–87
Nicene Creed, 81, 130
Nicodemus, 116

O

Oneness Pentecostalism, 60
only-begotten, 80, 87–88, 89, 180

P

Patripassianism, 62
Paul of Samosata, 103–104
Pharisees, 40
Plato, 127–128
Platonic Dualism, 13
Postmodernism, 90
praise, 45, 103, 107, 120, 136, 161,
    164

prayer, 8, 26, 45, 49, 54, 62, 65,
    66–67, 68, 73, 113, 138–139,
    143–144, 173, 176, 184
propitiation, 70–71
prototokos, 89
Pulcheria, 159–160

Q

Quest for Historical Jesus, 35
Qur'an, 22

R

Racovian Catechism, 104
resurrection, 15, 32, 40, 42, 78,
    117, 119, 134, 167, 168–169,
    170, 174, 179, 183
Robber Council, 159
Roman Empire, 21, 80

S

Sabellianism (see also Modalism),
    57, 66
Sabellius, 59, 61
sacrifice, 26, 50, 71, 141
salvation, 15, 26, 27, 48, 49–50,
    51, 81, 115, 118, 127, 143,
    167, 171, 173, 177, 180
Samaritan woman, 23, 28
Satan, 16–17, 119, 132, 137, 138–
    142, 145, 172
Schleiermacher, Friedrich, 32,
    33–34
Scribes, 43
sin, 25–26, 71–72
Solomon, 19
soul, 127, 134–135
Sozzini Brothers, 103–104
Spirit, 15

T

Temple, 19, 40, 64, 137, 139–
    140

temptation, 8, 16–17, 18, 37, 93,
    128–132, 137–142, 145–148,
    179
Tertullian, 57
The Lord of the Rings, 26, 98,
    156
Theodosius II, 158–159, 160
Theodotus, 103
Thomas, 40, 45
throne of God, 19, 45, 46–47, 172
Tree of Knowledge of Good and
    Evil, 167

Trinity, 57–58, 60–63, 65–69,
    72–73, 74, 80, 103–105, 118,
    177–178

U
Unitarianism, 104–105
Universalism, 105

W
Ware, Bruce, 109
WWJD, 17–18